TOGETHER ON THE WAY

A Theology of Ecumenism

Christopher J Ellis

The British Council of Churches
Inter-Church House
35-41 Lower Marsh
London SE1 7RL

ISBN 0 85169 209 5

Ref: 80 DEA

Published by
British Council of Churches
Inter-Church House
35-41 Lower Marsh
London SE1 7RL

Designed by Gooderham Bate
Printed by Design & Print, Shoreham-by-Sea, West Sussex

In memory of
the Reverend Idris Job Jones of Pontyclun,
my grandfather, who showed me the love of God.

And for Marilyn, with love.

ACKNOWLEDGEMENTS

This book has grown out of a shared experience of ecumenism as well as a personal commitment. I cannot name all the fellow pilgrims who have challenged and encouraged me along the way. However, I must put on record my affection and debt to Central Church, Swindon, and to the many friends committed to unity in Swindon and further afield.

This book would not have been possible if it were not for the sabbatical leave scheme of the Baptist Union of Great Britain. I would like to thank both the Baptist Union Ministry Department for making such a scheme possible and the students and staff of Bristol Baptist College who gave me their friendship and surrounded me with their fellowship for the term I was with them.

There have been moments when the road ahead seemed blocked and I would like to thank Rupert Davies and Roger Hayden for their friendship, guidance and encouragement. Many others have contributed advice and suggestions which is a reminder that theology should be a collaborative exercise, reflecting on experience and feeding off dialogue. Finally, I would like to thank my mother for her typing of the manuscript onto disc and Marilyn, my wife – for her readiness to cope while I was away on sabbatical, for her proof reading and patience, but especially for being herself.

The publisher is grateful to all who have given their permission for the reproduction of copyright material, the sources of which are acknowledged in the footnotes. Revised English Bible ©1989 by permission of the Oxford and Cambridge University Presses.

The author and the publisher are grateful also to the Whitely Trust for a grant towards the publication of this book.

PREFACE

At this time the member churches of the WCC are seeking 'a common understanding of the apostolic faith'. This involves reflection together on the faith as expressed in the creeds of the undivided church; explication of the faith in terms understandable today; and confession of that faith in relation to contemporary challenges to the Gospel. It also includes reflection together on the movement towards a deeper unity in mission as the churches draw on the diverse riches of their many traditions in order to witness and minister together in and to a world of many cultures.

Together on the Way: a Theology of Ecumenism is a welcome contribution to this process. It describes 'the ecumenical search' and its biblical basis in the fuller sense of the churches' involvement in the longing of divided and disrupted people for the reconciliation and wholeness of the human community. It covers 'the ecumenical debate' by looking at the multiple history of churches which since New Testament times have lived with both a common faith and a variety of distinctive ways of expressing it, and with the problems of discerning where the limits of diversity might lie as well as of recognising the truth wherever it may be found. It sees 'the ecumenical imperative' as a spiritual concern manifested in outward action and change, a movement both invisible and visible, a sign and foretaste of God's Kingdom towards which we are travelling as pilgrims together on the way. It refers both to the author's experience of local ecumenical projects in England and to the *Not Strangers But Pilgrims* Inter-Church Process in Britain.

I am happy to commend this excellent introduction to the rationale for ecumenism. I am delighted that our colleagues in the British Council of Churches are publishing it, and I endorse their confidence that Christopher J. Ellis has made a clear and timely contribution to the theological reflection and undergirding which the ecumenical process demands.

Emilio Castro
General Secretary
World Council of Churches

Geneva, March 1990

CONTENTS

Unless otherwise stated, all scripture quotations are from the Revised English Bible.

Chapter One

INTRODUCTION

The people gather. Standing shoulder to shoulder in the darkness of the Moscow church, grandmothers dressed in black lean against teenagers in jeans. A hush of expectation falls as all strain to hear the sound outside the church which will summon the arrival of Easter. Muffled voices are heard through the great door and, as the sounds of knocking and greeting die away, the paschal candle is lit. Steadily, the sea of faces becomes visible as the clutched candles are lit. Light is passed from one worshipper to another, and with each moment of the sharing of light, the jubilant greeting is exchanged. *Khristos voskrese! Christ is risen!: Voistinu voskrese! He is risen indeed!* Amidst the darkness of the night there is the flickering of candles. Christ is the light of the world and our lives are transfigured as we hold up our symbols of hope in a darkened world.[1]

Winter sunshine plays on the snow-covered roofs and brightens the grey slush which clogs pavement and gutter. As though competing with the sun, fluorescent tubes flash and glisten on dangling tinsel as shoppers stagger with parcels or stride, hands-in-pocket, from store to store. On the street-corner a uniformed group play the tidings of comfort and joy which hum from their trombones and tubas. The brass carols flow down the street and seep through the musak and the chatter. Red, bulging cheek empowering euphonium; cheerful cornet impersonating the angelic host and gloved hand shaking timbrel and collecting box – here is the church in worship, service and dogged proclamation.

The sun beats down on the corrugated roof of the shack, so the Peruvian slum-dwellers meet under the shade of a near-by wall – there are no trees here. The bible study begins with a sharing of news. Talk of drains and the collection of refuse is mixed with the reading of the Old Testament prophets. Here the yearning for a transformed world leads to a grateful reading of the Bible as God's promise to the poor. There is little liturgy but there is much hope born of faith.[2]

Faces peer from the Victorian gallery as a white-clad figure steps down into the baptistery water. A testimony of personal faith has been given and now the people sing as a new Christian is immersed with splashes of joy. The community celebrates its welcome and young faith is strengthened by its witness amongst loving friends.

Orchestra and choir soar on the beauty of the Schubert Mass. It is an Austrian Pentecost and the baroque cathedral resounds to classical celebration and crowded congregation. Tourists stand beside the villagers in their lederhosen and the shopkeepers in their aprons as the bishop preaches about the birthday of the church.

African rhythms syncopate the shade of a Kenyan church. Dancing and swirling songs spin a bond of fellowship and shared worship which ignores time, as the people rejoice at being together for the glory of God.

These pictures come from different continents. The people and the activities differ in their outward form and inner intent. And yet, there is something here which they all share – in each of these places we find 'the church'. The variety has come from different cultures and different histories; it has come from different personalities and different expectations. But each group would claim to represent the Church of God.

This in itself is a reminder of a fact of life within the church. There is variety and there is division. In a community where belief is important, it is natural that there will be strong views and partisan opinions. But it is also a community committed to the worship of a God of love who calls his people to live lives of love. So what are we to say about that aspect of the life of the church where some groups accept each other, while others claim to be *the* church, at best ignoring the others and at worst consigning them to outer darkness?

The modern ecumenical movement has developed amongst the churches during the twentieth century. In some places it has been a groundswell of changing attitudes while in other places it has meant negotiations towards the union of several national churches. Some have seen it as the work of the Spirit, while others have viewed the word *ecumenical* with extreme scepticism and its supporters with suspicion. Some have thought it to be only the concern of the church leaders while others have believed that its main purpose is in the local situation. So what is this Ecumenical Movement? Where has it come from and where is it going?

A catalogue of events cannot adequately present a history or explain a movement. However, this movement has moved on a number levels and each has affected the other. To describe international conferences is only to provide part of a story, but those conferences are important for they have widened the sharing of a vision and enabled leaders to meet. Without a change in attitudes and the growth of friendship at the local level, there would be no movement, but the Church is more than the local congregation and the local church is often hindered by barriers that can only be dismantled at a national or international level.

The International Scene

The church is part of the world and will be influenced by movements and trends in the wider world. We need to look carefully when trends within the church mirror trends within society and we must test these trends against our understanding of the gospel. Sometimes we will be chastened by what we discover, while at other times we will claim to find in these wider trends evidence of the leading of the Holy Spirit. Some will see evidence of such mirrored trends in the ecumenical movement, where its international development seems to reflect that growing awareness of living in one world which has been a part of the Twentieth Century experience. Improved transport and communication systems, together with imperial expansion and the horrors of industrialized warfare, have led to international peace movements. These have been concerned with the promotion of understanding, the reinforcing of diplomacy as a means of resolving disputes and the co-ordination of relief programmes across national boundaries. The United Nations, the World Health Organization and UNESCO are secular expressions of a growing international awareness, just as the ecumenical movement is an ecclesiastical expression. Other ecclesiastical examples would include the world confessional bodies such as the Baptist World Alliance and the Lutheran World Federation. This link between secular and ecclesiastical trends can be seen clearly in the initiative of the Orthodox Church after the First World War. Inspired by the founding of the League of Nations, the Holy Synod of the Church of Constantinople issued in 1920 an invitation 'unto all the churches everywhere' to form a league of churches.[3]

While its roots go further back, the modern beginnings of the ecumenical movement are usually identified with the international *Edinburgh Missionary Conference* of 1910. Its main purpose was to do with missions and missionaries, but it inspired many to work for unity between the churches. The main insight of the conference was 'that a disunited church was a denial of the gospel and a major scandal in Christian mission.'[4]

Inspired by this, three international movements began: the *International Missionary Council, Faith and Order* concerned with doctrine and *Life and Work*, concerned with promoting justice and peace. In 1948, *Faith and Order* and *Life and Work* came together to form the *World Council of Churches* (WCC) and they were joined by the *International Missionary Council* in 1961.

An important feature of the WCC is the part that churches from the Third World have come to play in its life. Mission is no longer seen as Western

Christians taking the gospel to other countries, but as the mutual support and inspiration of the world church for the witness of God's people in each place. Theology, mission and spirituality have been greatly enriched by the widening of the ecumenical movement to embrace a variety of cultures as well as a variety of denominations.

Although the Roman Catholic Church participates in *Faith and Order*, since 1948 a major commission within the World Council of Churches, it is not a member of the WCC. Nonetheless, its ecumenical involvement has been steadily growing since the Second Vatican Council (1962-1965). At the end of the council various ancient anathemas against the Eastern churches were withdrawn and the official statements of that church have become more eirenic and less threatening to others. However, while we can rejoice at the involvement of the Roman Catholic Church, we must also recognize that this inevitably means that some solutions already arrived at by Protestants will need to be reworked and the whole process of unity becomes more complicated.

There are no easy answers. Consensus might unite a few strands of the church which start life close together anyway, but it needs more than this to unite the whole people of God. The challenge of Roman Catholic participation can be mirrored by the challenges of various Protestant and Charismatic groups: if we see richness in the variety of heritage and the diversity of faith and witness, there is little to be gained by regretting the breadth or spectrum as an inconvenience. In human terms, ecumenists often seem to be faced with the stark alternative of a few moving forward rapidly or many moving forward slowly. This is one of the practical dilemmas of the ecumenical movement.

Alongside all this, there are, at the national and international levels, groups such as the YMCA and various peace organizations which unite Christians because of their concern for a particular issue. To this we can add other bodies such as the Evangelical Alliance, which is a forum for Christians to co-operate across denominational boundaries on a platform of evangelical orthodoxy, but where many of the members are suspicious of 'official ecumenism' for a variety of reasons.

National Attempts

At the national level ecumenism has taken two main forms. First, in many countries there are national councils of churches which provide a meeting place for the exchange of views and the sharing of fellowship as well as for setting up agencies which can act on behalf of the churches.

Secondly, there have been attempts at uniting various denominations at a national level. Internationally, the best known are the churches of South and North India, while in Britain the United Reformed Church is the result of an amalgamation of three national denominations. Wider attempts at union in Britain have been less successful. The Anglican/Methodist Schemes of 1969 and 1972 and the Covenant proposals up to 1982, attempting to involve five denominations, each failed to gain the necessary majority in the Church of England General Synod.

In the late 1980's the *'Not Strangers But Pilgrims' Inter-Church Process* offered hope to many in the British churches. While the *union* schemes have been the attempts of a few to move a long way, the *Inter-Church Process* has involved a breadth of Christian expression, from Black-led Pentecostal to Roman Catholic, which may offer more hope in the long term. However, the challenge of those churches who have managed to unite remains[5] – reconciliation is costly and we have to offer all that we have and are to God if he is to renew his people.

Local Unity

At the local level the ecumenical movement has taken a number of forms. First, there are local *councils of churches* which enable Christians to meet each other, unite for worship and act jointly in certain areas. Secondly, there are the less formal links between individuals and groups which happen as a result of the changing climate towards openness, rather than because of organized structures. Thirdly, there are organizations with a particular concern, such as local hospices and world development groups, which draw members from various churches because they have a shared concern.

Then there are *Local Ecumenical Projects*, which are local experiments in unity approved by the denominations. These can range from a local covenant of churches in a market town to a newly-formed, ecumenical congregation in a new housing area, or the amalgamation of several long-established churches in a town centre.

Finally, there are ecumenical housegroups which meet for fellowship, study and prayer. It is reckoned that in Britain as a whole, close on a million people were involved in the 'Lent 86' discussion groups and this groundswell has been seen as an important factor in the promising beginnings of the Inter Church Process.

Vision and Reflection

Movements cannot be organized or orchestrated from the centre. Initiatives can be taken which will inspire, events can happen which will provide symbols, but there is more to it than that. Those committed to the ecumenical movement believe that it is the work of the Spirit of God. What follows here is an attempt to examine that claim.

This is a partisan book. It is written by someone committed to the search for the unity of the church. It is intended both for those who share this concern and for those who do not. It is easy to be impressed by many of the people within the ecumenical movement, but often the same people would be unable to provide a coherent defence of their involvement. Many good people will follow their noses, they will act in a certain way because 'their hearts are in the right places'. If questioned, they would speak about their inner conviction that God is a God of unity rather than discord, that the arguments and conflicts of the past need to be healed, and they will point to the need of the church 'to get its act together' in the face of increasing secularism. The most important aim of this book is to provide a series of theological reflections on the question, 'Why is unity important?'. It may well be that 'gut feelings' are more important than theological reflection, but my concern here is to provide a framework within which all kinds of people may see the validity of these hopes and endeavours.

The ecumenical movement has its fair share of critics, its fair share of opponents and its fair share of discouragement. When these are encountered we need to be able to reflect on *why* the whole business is important so that we don't give up. This book is not intended as a treatise for the experts but is offered as survival rations for the troops. It is written in the firm conviction that a disunited church is a poor witness to the gospel of Christ. The search for unity is not an optional extra for a few enthusiasts, but an imperative placed upon all Christians by the gospel of reconciliation and the fundamental conviction that all Christian action should be motivated by love. Thus the ecumenical debate is a debate about faithfulness.

There are other movements and processes in our world and we must be aware of them. There is a growing impetus towards fundamentalism in both the religious and political spheres. The desire for safety and dogmatic assertion is a force to be reckoned with, within the church as well as further afield. These are challenges for the ecumenical movement to face. How might we reach an understanding of commitment that is not dogmatic? How do we cope with the narrow line between tolerance and apathy? Is ecumenism only for the liberal mind or is its appeal more comprehensive than that?

It can already be seen that the issues raised easily spill over into issues for the whole community and not only the church. This is healthy because the church must be concerned with the whole of humanity and not just its internal affairs.

Reconciliation isn't only on the agenda of the church but is on the agenda of the whole human race. The polarization of communities and traditions, the violence of language, the widening gap between communities, are not only ecumenical issues for the church, they are ecumenical issues for everyone.

The reader who consults the table of contents will see that what follows is offered in three parts.

Part One begins with an examination of the word *ecumenical* and locates its meaning in the world as well as the church. There follows a study of the life and mission of the church which identifies the people of God as a people seeking to embody those values and hopes which God has offered us in

Christ. The *life* of the church is to be found in the *purpose* of the church and this is to be seen in its mission in and for the world. The ultimate ecumenical vision is seen as a part of that hope which longs for the whole universe to be caught up in the redeeming purposes of God.

The other chapter in this part traces a number of biblical themes – peace, fellowship, reconciliation, unity, oneness and love – and argues that these provide a mandate for the ecumenical search.

Part Two begins with an historical study which claims that there never was a golden age of unity in the church and that even the New Testament portrays a church enriched and endangered by great diversity. That in turn leads to questioning *how* this variety might be held in a united communion and the focus turns to the Lordship of Christ. This is re-inforced by the following chapter which offers arguments from theological method, especially the limitations of theological language, which necessitate the holding of differing insights in tension.

Part Three explores the borderland between theory and practice in which the question *how?* begins to emerge and take shape. It argues that only *visible* unity is an adequate unity and bases this on the nature of the church, the doctrine of creation and the proclamation of the Kingdom of God. It is followed by a chapter on mission which looks at the issue of credibility and seeks to reflect theologically upon it. This brings us full circle with a statement about the relationship of church to gospel. The final chapter looks for some sign-posts for the future. The *how?* question is taken further, but the reader who is looking for a prediction on the detail of future unity will be disappointed. The task of this book is to develop a *theological* basis for the unity search, not offer predetermined solutions for a path that is supposed to be a path of faith.

We must all give account of the hope that is in us. As a personal testimony, I have to say that I have glimpsed unity. The vision has been partial and through a glass darkly, but this work is undertaken in the hope that such glimpses can be signs for the future. Here is no clear blueprint for the church in the Twentyfirst Century. The purpose is not one of prediction or the provision of a programme. The concern is to give account of that hope and to reflect on it using the resources of scripture, tradition and experience.

I believe that the church has been entrusted with a ministry of recon-ciliation. We shall explore how reconciliation within the church relates to reconciliation within the wider world. *Entrusted* suggests that this has come from God and the conviction is here confessed that unity in the church and unity for the world is the will of God – that there is a divine imperative which cannot be ignored. The belief and the commitment are stated at the outset – the rest is an attempt to explore and justify this commitment to ecumenism.

Notes

1. A moving eye witness account of a Moscow Paschal vigil may be found in M. Bordeaux, 'Risen Indeed' (London) 1983 pp41-42.

2. For a description of a Basic Christian Community meeting in a Peruvian favella see D. Winter, 'Hope in Captivity' (London) 1977 pp33-38.

3. J. Matthews, 'The Unity Scene' (London) 1986 p19, though the correct date for the call to the world was January 1920.

4. See Matthews p19. For a full treatment of Edinburgh 1910 and what flowed from it see R. Rouse and S.C. Neill (ed.), 'A History of the Ecumenical Movement, vol 1 (1517-1948)' (Geneva) 3rd edition 1986 pp353-542.

5. See M. Kinnamon and T.F. Best (ed.), 'Called to be One: United Churches and the Ecumenical Movement' (Geneva) 1985.

THE ECUMENICAL SEARCH

Chapter Two

SONG OF CREATION

When some people hear the word *ecumenical* they 'think big'. In the local church, they might think of 'that united service' in the Week of Prayer for Christian Unity. On the other hand, 'the ecumenical movement' might suggest a coming together, such as a local council of churches or even the World Council of Churches. In this last example, size has taken a global dimension and we seem to be in the same league as 'power blocks' and 'multi-national companies'. So, for some, ecumenism can mean being part of a large machine or organisation, part of a mass movement where the individual and the local congregation are swamped and diminished.

But is this true? It may be a correct description of how *some* people understand ecumenism, but is it what ecumenism is about? Talk about unity often seems to suggest amalgamation and adding pieces together. How should the ecumenical movement relate to the world and what is the relationship between the local and the global?

How Ecumenical is 'Ecumenical'?
The word 'ecumenical' comes from the Greek word *OIKOUMENE* [1]. Over the years it has had a variety of meanings and some of these are important for our understanding of its use today. Of course, we must use the *history* of a word with care. The meaning of a word is often more related to its modern use than to its etymology and history. But when an 'old' word is 're-discovered' and given a new, or at least modern, meaning, then we are justified in searching for those older nuances which have made possible its contemporary development and acceptance.

The Greek *OIKOUMENE* literally means 'the inhabited world'. [2] In time it came to have the additional meaning of 'the civilised world', and by the time of Alexander the Great it became equated with the idea of empire. These two meanings are reflected in the Bible. In the Septuagint, the Greek translation of the Old Testament which was widely used at the time when the New Testament was being written, Psalm 24.1 is rendered:

> '*To the Lord belong the earth* (GE: earth, land) *and everything in it, the world* (OIKOUMENE) *and all its inhabitants.*'

The other meaning is present in Luke 2.1, where the decree of Caesar Augustus is that the whole OIKOUMENE, ie. the whole empire, should be enrolled.

However, the dominant meaning seems to be 'the whole inhabited world', as in Matthew 24.14:

> 'And this gospel of the kingdom will be proclaimed throughout the earth (OIKOUMENE) as a testimony to all nations.'

Over the centuries the word also came to refer to the *church* in its world-wide expression and, with the adoption of Christianity as the state religion of the Roman Empire, the references to church and empire became very close. In time, the *Ecumenical Councils* were convened by the emperor, but it would probably be fair to say that they are regarded as 'ecumenical' for two reasons. First, the bishops who were present represented the whole church (in the known world) and, secondly, the teaching of these councils was recognized by the whole church. [3] Eventually, the imperial meaning of *OIKOUMENE* began to drop away so that the word came to refer to a council or a belief which was regarded as 'orthodox' rather than 'universal'.

In the Twentieth Century the movement seeking unity for the church has taken this word and applied it to itself. [4] In doing so it has not intended to appropriate all the meanings and nuances of a word which has developed over two and a half thousand years. Ultimately, it is the self understanding of the movement which is important rather than the etymology of its title. However, this brief survey should help us to see which nuances are relevant to the modern ecumenical movement and which are not.

In its modern use the word *ecumenical* is not meant to carry the imperial meanings, nor the sense of church and state which were a part of the Byzantine world. Nor can the assemblies of the World Council of Churches be seen as *ecumenical councils*, for they neither represent the whole church (for example the Roman Catholic Church is not in membership) nor are their pronouncements authoritative in the way that the early ecumenical councils' statements have been widely recognized as being. That is not to say that there will not be a time in the future when a council *beyond* the World Council of Churches may be rightly seen as an ecumenical council, but that time is not yet.

The 1937 Oxford 'Life and Work' conference gave the first official definition of the word *ecumenical*.

> 'The term ecumenical refers to the expression within history of the given unity of the church. The thought and action of the church are ecumenical, in so far as they attempt to realise the "Una Sancta", the fellowship of Christians who acknowledge the one Lord.' [5]

So the first modern meaning of the word refers to that movement and conviction which believes that it is God's will that his church should be one. Related to this meaning is the confessing of Jesus Christ as a common Lord, a nurturing of fellowship between Christians of difference traditions and a concern for joint action in the world. Undergirding this is the belief that this unity should have a visible, social expression as the ecclesiastical dimension of Christ's reconciling work.

The second modern meaning which has been embraced in recent years is the word's literal meaning of 'the whole inhabited world'. Here *ecumenical* refers to an assembly of representatives from all over the world, in their cultural, racial, social and political diversity. This is an enriching dimension of the ecumenical movement and one which is often missed, despite its closeness to the original meaning of *OIKOUMENE*. The diversity of cultures and experiences is not to be flattend out in a cultural sameness but is to be a celebration of the glorious variety of God's creation. Linked with this meaning is the realization that reconciliation is something desperately needed by the whole world.

In an address to the Vancouver Assembly of the World Council of Churches, Philip Potter reflected on the word *OIKOUMENE* and the related word *oikos*, meaning house:

'It is the means by which the churches that form . . . the house, the oikos of God, are seeking so to live and witness before all peoples that the whole oikoumene may become the oikos of God through the crucified and risen Christ in the power of the life-giving Spirit.' [6]

The Earth is The Lord's

Because of this, we can see that to define *ecumenical* as 'inter-church' or even 'the search for church unity' is to devalue both the word and the ecumenical movement below acceptable limits. We can say that the first task for the churches (in the sense of the first task to be tackled) is reconciliation, leading to a form of life which outwardly expresses that reconciliation. But this is not enough: we must go on and say that the first task (in the sense of the first task in order of priority) is the search for reconciliation in the world. 'God so loved the *world* that he gave his only Son . . .' We shall see, time and again, how unity in the world and in the church are inseparable – here, in the word 'ecumenical' itself, we are confirmed in that belief. This is not really because of an argument based on the history of the word, but because of the very nature of the gospel itself. The world comes first. The church is called and sent out into the *OIKOUMENE*. The church is gathered, that it might be used as a sign for the whole inhabited world.

The link between the unity of the church and the unity of humanity cannot be stressed too much. The statement at the 1968 Uppsala assembly of the World Council of Churches claimed, 'The church is bold in speaking of itself as the sign of the coming unity of mankind'. [7] The Faith and Order Commission had a programme entitled 'The Unity of the Church and the Unity of Humankind'. This has now been replaced by a programme entitled 'The Unity of the

Church and the Renewal of Human Community'. In all this we see the same concern for claiming ecumenism as a seamless robe.

If we look in upon the church, with our backs to the world, and simply try to join the various parts of the ecclesiastical machinery together, we shall betray our mission. But more than that, we shall find the unity of the church frustratingly elusive, for it is based on the one who is Lord of all and not only Lord of the church. Similarly, if we neglect the church and simply try to effect reconciliation in the world, we will cease to have any credibility as reconcilers and we shall have no resources as healers. Church and world are linked in an historical partnership that cannot be transformed by only tackling one side or the other. The church is *in* the world and the church is *for* the world. The church is *from* the world and the church is sent *into* the world. We can only use the word *ecumenical* within the context of these missionary and sacramental statements.

Creation and redemption belong together. Redemption is the making good of that which has been created and has been distorted by sin. Redemption is achieved by God acting in Christ and *through* the Body of Christ *within* the world. Ultimately, our argument about the word *ecumenical* is not to be based on the history of the word, or even the way it is used in the contemporary ecumenical movement. Our argument is to be based on the eternal realities of salvation history: the calling of a people, the sharing of our humanity and the sacrificial suffering of the servant for the redemption of the world. This is why *ecumenical* means both the healing of divisions within the church and the faithful obedience of God's people, in and for and with the world.

At the Lima meeting of the Faith and Order Commission in 1982, the group discussing unity reported:

> 'On this pilgrimage there is always for Christians a double command – to search for what God wants for his church and to search for what he intends for the whole inhabited creation, the OIKOUMENE. These can never be separated, for the church exists as a human community called in and for the world as a whole. They are not the same command . . . Yet, in every situation, the search for the oneness and wholeness of the human community has much to contribute to the search for the oneness and wholeness of Christ's church; it is also always true that obedience in the search for oneness and wholeness of the church, in her specific calling to be the body of Christ, will sooner or later contribute to the search for true human community . . . The dynamism of this inter-relatedness is the leading of the Holy Spirit, restlessly guiding his people through all limitations and all sin towards the kingdom.' [8]

Yet, despite this emphasis, we must affirm something very important about the word *ecumenical*. It does not only mean 'big', just as the word *world* doesn't only mean 'big'. *World* can refer to what we find on our door step and what we face within our hearts, as well as 'planet earth'. In the same way, the ecumenical movement is not a distant, mass movement which dwarfs the individual person and the local community. The ecumenical movement is wherever there is living reconciliation in the church, wherever boundaries are transcended and barriers broken down. Here the word *ecumenical* operates rather like the word *catholic* or *missionary*. The *catholic* church is not only the universal church, but also its local expression wherever believers come together in worship and witness. The missionary task is not just something that leads people to foreign countries, but is a task for each local congregation in the world on its doorstep.

We must not allow *reconciliation* to become an abstract word. There are very practical needs in the world and in the church, where the spirit of reconciliation is needed to heal the fears which destroy relationships and the wounds that hurt. Because of this, the word *ecumenical* must also be a local word, even when it has universal significance. The incarnation was very particular and very local. It meant the eternal Word taking First Century, Jewish flesh and being crucified on a very particular cross in a particular city on a particular day. Yet here we see the pivot of God's saving action for the universe. The universal significance of the cross is only possible because of its actual, historical happening. In the same kind of way, the ecumenical movement can have no global or universal significance unless it takes flesh in real, local events and communities.

Lukas Vischer, a former director of the Faith and Order Commission, wrote at the time of the Uppsala assembly of the World Council of Churches:

> 'The church is one people in many places. It is not a structure to which the congregations are subordinated, and the individual local congregations are not parts in the sense that they form the church only when they are joined to make a whole. Since Christ is wholly and directly present in each individual part, each individual part is church; Christ's presence is not transmitted to the individual church by some totality to which it is subordinate. The church in Corinth **is** the body of Christ; it is not merely a member of the body of Christ. This does not mean that the churches do not belong together. Precisely because Christ is present in all of them, they are closely connected and must also prove this bond. But the universal church is a fellowship of local churches and can appear only as such a fellowship.'[9]

And Behold

Here is a vision of reality which is both particular and universal, near and distant. Just as William Blake invited us to see eternity in a grain of sand, so we need to have a cosmic setting for our local concerns and, at the same time, an earthing of all our wider imaginings. As we shall see in chapter 7, belief in a creator means that we see the world in a certain way. We see the stuff of the universe and its history as being invested with eternal significance.

There have been times in the history of Christian thought when the material world has been devalued. It has been seen as essentially evil, or just the stage of a Creator God who leads us to identify this world as a part of his purpose, to recognize the stuff of creation as divine gift and to acknowledge the destruction of its *shalom*, its peace, as a sin to be named and a wound to be healed. The biblical testimony is clear that there is an 'ecology of salvation', because neither our existence in this world, nor our destiny hereafter, is disembodied.

> *'To the Lord belong the earth and everything in it,*
> *the world and all its inhabitants.*
> *For it was he who founded it on the seas*
> *and planted it firm on the waters beneath.*
> *Who may go up the mountain of the Lord?*
> *Who may stand in his holy place?'   (Psalm 24.1-3)*

Such an affirmation about the world is the setting for our worship, because it enables us to approach God not only as *Lord* but as *Giver*. The material universe and human destiny are linked, both in the stories of creation in Genesis 1 and 2, and in the biblical visions of the future. So the anonymous prophet of the exile in Babylon described Israel's return to the promised land as a new exodus – an event in history, but one that was to be accompanied by cosmic rejoicing:

> *'You will go out with joy and be led forth in peace.*
> *Before you mountains and hills will break into cries of joy,*
> *and all the trees in the countryside will clap their hands.'   (Isaiah 55.12)*

The subsequent return of the exiles to Palestine, in fact, was to be far less glamorous, and we will be forgiven for seeing in the prophet's description of the future a certain amount of 'poetic hype'. However, this linking of the earth with the fortunes of humanity is clear in Genesis 1.28-31, where stewardship is the theme, and also in the idea of *shalom*[10] which lies behind many of the Old Testament laws concerning the care of the environment. (eg. Leviticus 25.1-7 and Deuteronomy 22.6-7,9).

So it is not surprising that, when we turn to the New Testament, the visions of the future speak both of humanity resurrected by the power of God in Christ and of the whole universe being transformed. Paul's argument in 1 Corinthians 15, about the resurrection of the body, suggests both continuity and discontinuity. While in verse 40 he speaks of different kinds of bodies, in verses 43 and 44 he still sees the future as *the future of what has died*, rather than something completely different:

> *'Sown in humiliation, it is raised in glory; sown in weakness, it is raised in power;*
> *sown a physical body, it is raised a spiritual body.'*

The vision of Revelation is of 'a new heaven and a new earth' – again the continuity and the discontinuity of God's action. Christians will differ in their views of the eternal destiny of those who die without faith in Christ, but the glimpses of a transformed creation lead us to a comprehensive hope in the loving purposes of God:

> 'He has made known to us his secret purpose, in accordance with the plan which he determined beforehand in Christ, to be put into effect when the time was ripe: namely that the universe, everything in heaven and on earth, might be brought into a unity in Christ.' (Ephesians 1.8f.)

Whatever our speculation about that future, the role of the church is clear. It is to proclaim the gospel to all people, to witness to what God has done in Christ so that his purpose for the world may be fulfilled.

> 'Full authority in heaven and on earth has been committed to me. Go therefore to all nations and make them my disciples; baptize them in the name of the Father and the Son and the Holy Spirit, and teach them to observe all that I have commanded you. I will be with you always, to the end of time.' (Matthew 28.18-20)

Not only is Christ the one who commissions and the one who accompanies, he is also the one through whose death and resurrection the nations will be gathered:

> 'Now is the hour of judgement for this world; now shall the prince of this world be driven out. And when I am lifted up from the earth I shall draw everyone to myself.' (John 12.31f)

The 'Theology of Hope' has become an important emphasis in recent decades.[11] Hope for the world places the church in its true context as a sacrament and sign of the coming Kingdom. Here is no easy optimism, for this hope is founded on God and his promises, especially that divine act which is both fulfilment and future promise: the resurrection of Jesus of Nazareth. This hope for the world is a disturbing thing because it shows us the *nature* of reality by showing us its *future*, what it *ought* to be. It makes us dissatisfied with the way things are and goads us on in the faithful anticipation here and now of that which is yet to come in Christ.

The church is called to point to the future by living in the present. We are called to live God's future, revealed in the life and death and resurrection of Jesus Christ, now, in the midst of this decaying and distorted creation. This life is the life of the Spirit of God working in the world and in the church. It is the very opposite of triumphalism, for it can only produce the agonies of crucifixion and the painful struggles of childbirth. The future brought into the present is how Paul understands the raising of Jesus (1 Corinthians 15.20), but before this could happen he had to live the Kingdom of God within a world that did not acknowledge God's reign. This was the tension which led to the cross, and it is this same cross which disciples are invited to carry. Thus the church's calling is *in* the world and *for* the world, but it is promised death as well as rejoicing.

> 'The created universe is waiting with eager expectation for God's sons to be revealed. It was made subject to frustration, not of its own choice but by the will of him who subjected it, yet with the hope that the universe itself is to be freed from the shackles of mortality and is to enter upon the glorious liberty of the children of God. Up to the present, as we know, the whole created universe in all its parts groans as if in the pangs of childbirth. What is more, we also, to whom the Spirit is given as the firstfruits of the harvest to come, are groaning inwardly while we look forward eagerly to our adoption, our liberation from mortality. It was with this hope that we were saved.' (Romans 8.19-24)

Celebration and Sign

> 'It is the day of resurrection.
> Let us be glorious in splendour for the celebration,
> and let us embrace one another.
> Let us speak also, brothers and sisters, to those that hate us
> and in the resurrection let us forgive all things;
> and so let us cry:
> Christ has risen from the dead,
> by death trampling upon death,
> and has bestowed life to those in tombs.' [12]

This Orthodox, Easter hymn reminds us that, whatever the time of year, whatever the place, whoever the people, the church exists because of Easter; it lives in the light of Easter and it is called to celebrate Easter even, or perhaps especially, in the valley of the shadow of death. 'We are the Easter people and 'Hallelujah' is our song.' [13] But what kind of people does this make us?

Easter is, of course, the celebration of the resurrection of Christ. It is the feast of victory, when we rejoice that death has been vanquished and our future destiny is shown to us in the one who was dead but is now alive. Life has overcome death, good has overcome evil, love has overcome hate. Or has it? Death still engulfs us, hate oppresses and distorts the life of the world. One man may have been raised, but swollen bellies still announce their harvest of death. Is the celebration of the church an escape from reality or an announcing of what is real amidst the shadows of a struggling world?

We need to remind ourselves about Easter itself. The message of the biblical witness is *not* that Jesus rose from the dead. He was dead and buried and there was no power left. The Messiah was a 'has-been' who cried 'It is finished', and then *he* was finished. The biblical witness is not of some superman, who lay in wait in the tomb for the appointed third day when he could spring out to surprise the sentries and bewilder the disciples.

The witness of the Bible is not that Jesus rose from the dead but that God raised him to life again. The one who was dead and buried was powerless, for he had submitted everything on the cross of his faithfulness. The resurrection was thus not the act of power of a divine champion, but the act of vindication of a loving and just God. When God raised Jesus to life, he was saying 'Amen' to the claims of his life and his teaching. On the Mount of Transfiguration the disciples heard a voice saying, 'This is my beloved Son; listen to him.' (Mark 9.7). Peter preached this to the Jerusalem crowds on the day of Pentecost:

> 'Let all Israel then accept as certain that God has made this same Jesus, whom you crucified, both Lord and Messiah.' (Acts 2.36)

This is important not only for our understanding of the significance of Easter but for our understanding of the nature and purpose of the church. If God's raising of Jesus was a vindication of all that he had done and stood for, and a revelation of who he was, then the resurrection must also be seen as an underlining of the values of the Kingdom which were embodied in Jesus. The resurrection then becomes a divine revelation. Jesus announced the arrival of the Kingdom, demonstrated the Kingdom and lived the Kingdom. By his death on the cross, the powers of darkness and death, of hatred and fear, sought to extinguish his life. They succeeded. The resurrection is God's kindling of that light again, an act of new creation which we can identify as an act of God because we recognize the marks of Jesus in the risen Lord and his renewed disciples.

The church exists because of Easter. If the resurrection had not happened, the dispirited disciples would have returned from whence they came, ridiculed and pitied. The dream would have soured and disappeared. But the coming of the Christ was not a dream so much as a vision, incarnate in the one who lived out the Kingdom. The teaching *was* true, the claims *were* still valid, the forgiveness *was* real. So the church began under the shadow of a cross, but in the light of a resurrection. The church began as a group of people who had encountered the claims of Jesus and who, in the light of his resurrection, were empowered to try and live those claims themselves. If Jesus was the living claim of the reign of God, so his disciples were called to continue the incarnation of the coming Kingdom. If his new life was the firstfruit of those who are raised from the dead, then the new life of his followers was to be the continuing firstfruit of God's recreating power. The Spirit at work in their lives was the Spirit of Jesus, and their identity as a community had meaning in so far as they were the people of the Christ −Christians.

The Easter People

If Easter was the vindication of the one who was claimed by his followers to be the Messiah, then we can affirm that the church is called to be a *messianic* community. If the Kingdom was announced and lived in Jesus, then it is to be announced and lived in his followers. Because of this we can claim that the church is a sign of the Kingdom and a foretaste of its coming glory. [14]

There are two important ecumenical implications of all this which affect our understanding of the church and the way in which ecumenism is to be seen as central to the church and not merely peripheral.

First, if the church is called to be a messianic community living in the light of Easter, then we must see this as another way of expressing *the Lordship of Christ*. We shall see in chapters 4 and 5 how a shared confession of 'Jesus is Lord' was a unifying factor for the church in the time of the New Testament, and how it can be the same today. What we must recognise and ensure is that this shared affirmation is not merely a creed of convenience, nor an ad hoc, unifying formula to cobble together a broken church. The Lordship of Christ is the very foundation of the church and without it the church would cease to be the church. Unless the church confesses Christ as Lord, it ceases to be the church. More than that, the very fact that it does not live up to this confession causes a tension between its historical existence, its performance, and its calling and vision. So the very foundation of the church in the Lordship of Christ is that which draws its differing parts and diverse members together – but it is also the very thing which puts the disunity of the church under judgement.

This is vital in our theological reflection on the ecumenical movement. We shall marshal arguments from the biblical witnesses, we shall argue from the relationship of ecumenism to mission and from the nature of the gospel. Here, at the beginning of our search, we are arguing that the ecumenical movement is a movement which leads the church *towards* the fulfilment of its very being. If the church confesses 'Jesus Christ is Lord', and if this means that because of Easter we are now called to live the values, promises and hopes embodied in Jesus, then the same confession which *constitutes* the church also *unites* it.

Many people and institutions feel threatened by the ecumenical movement because they believe that it threatens the church by seeking to change it from its traditional form to something new. That it promises something new cannot be denied, but the ecumenical movement also claims to call the church to become more truly itself. By confessing 'Jesus is Lord' and by living that lordship in all its forgiving and reconciling power, the church will be led to a healing of its own divisions as well as a strengthening of its witness to Jesus Christ, the hope of the world.

Secondly, if the church is called to be a messianic community, the confession 'Jesus is Lord' must be more than a verbal confession which provides a basis for doctrinal agreement, or a convergence. The confession should also be a *manifesto* for a messianic lifestyle. If Jesus *is* Lord, then the church must seek to announce good news to the poor, release to prisoners and sight to the blind.

If Jesus *is* Lord then the Church must seek to announce and live the forgiving grace of God and the liberating love of the one who is the Good Shepherd. To *live* this gospel is to build an open community where the waifs and strays are welcome and where the trends of living are towards unity rather than division. The Good Shepherd promised one flock and one shepherd (John 10.16), but we must remember that the one flock is made possible because of the one shepherd. The 'Lordship of Christ' is a foundation of the ecumenical movement not because it is a simplified and uncontentious creed, but because the reality of that Lordship draws together the Easter people who seek to live in the power of his resurrection.

This embodying of the priorities of Jesus in the life of the church should be a sign of hope to the world. It is in this way that examples of reconciliation and unity within the church are also signs of hope to the wider world, for they point to the promise of God that all things will be united in Christ. So the unity of the church becomes a sign of hope pointing to the renewal and unity of humanity. Jesus Christ has shown us our future, the destiny which God has in store for us. The resurrection is God's vindication of this, telling those who have the eyes of faith that this is indeed their future. As a result, the church is called to live humanity's future *now*. To be the Easter people we must live the life of the Lord of Easter – that the world might believe:

> 'I give you a new commandment: love one another; as I have loved you, so you are to love one another. If there is this love among you, then everyone will know that you are my disciples.' (John 13.34f)

But just as Christ's living of the Kingdom led to his death, so the church must be warned that faithfulness to the Kingdom will still lead to crucifixion in a world such as ours. To be the Easter people is not plain sailing, nor is it a triumphal band-wagon. Easter leads back to a cross. To live God's *shalom*, his peace, now, to live forgiveness now, to seek his reconciliation now, to live his love now – this is a costly calling and it is only God's forgiveness which keeps the frail human beings who make up the church in touch with the reality they seek to live.

The Lordship of Christ is not only something to be lived out, it is a confession which provides a means of grace in worship. Because Jesus is Lord, the church submits to the Bible, the testimony of those who point us to the Lord of the church. Through the Scriptures, we recognize our own frailty and sin, the compromises and the contradictions of a sinful humanity which is still called to be an incarnation of God's gracious gospel. The reading and studying of the Word which point us to *the* Word is a means of grace which reminds us of our Lord. It not only reminds us *who* our Lord is, but it reminds us *what* our Lord is like. This in turn makes us face again our calling as his people, even amidst the broken promises and all-too-human failures.

But we are given even more than this, for the church which is called to be a sacrament of grace for the world is in turn itself given sacraments of grace. These are to enable the church to be the church – *sacraments to enable us to be a sacrament.*

So baptism into the death and resurrection of Christ is an initiation into the life of the Easter people whose identity is found in the one who is raised to be Lord of the church. Baptism is more than a confession of faith, but it is at least that, for in baptism we publicly acknowledge 'the crown rights of the redeemer', and join the community of those who share his Lordship. Because baptism enables us to encounter the absolute claims of the Lord of life, it also enables the church to face those same claims which are its calling. In facing the claims of its Lord, the church is encouraged to seek the unity which comes from sharing a common baptism in a common Lord.

Because we find the Lordship of Christ to be undergirding the sacrament of baptism, we find a unifying theme even for those Christians who do not practise baptism, for we share the one Lord. Although the Society of Friends and the Salvation Army do not practise baptism as a sacrament of water, their living the Lordship of Christ can be seen to be a baptism in the one Lord, and therefore something which binds them to other parts of the church.[15] Because the sacraments are given to the church to enable the church to be a sacrament, baptism is important not because it might be seen to secure personal salvation, but because it enables the church to *be* the church through the Lordship of Christ. As well as confessing its faith at a service of baptism, the church also announces the good news of the one who laid down his life for us and whom God raised to life.

In a similar way, the Eucharist is a sacrament which enables the church to be a sacrament for the world. Again, the acts of eating and drinking are a reaffirmation of our baptismal vows, a confessing anew of the Lordship of Christ. The saving activity of God in the cross and the resurrection provides the focus for this meal. The bread is broken and we are faced with the agony of sacrificial love. The bread is broken and shared and we are faced with the calling to be one people. We eat of one loaf and are faced with the reality of living as the Body of Christ. All this is in the shadow of a cross and in the light of Easter, for the eucharist is the celebration of the Easter people and the sacrament which enables them to live the Lordship of Christ. We are reminded of our calling at the same time as we encounter the redeeming love of the crucified Saviour. We are called to be a people of hope as we eat of the flesh and drink of the blood of the one who is the hope of the world.

> 'We announce your death and proclaim your resurrection, Lord Jesus; gather all your people into your Kingdom when you come in glory.'[16]

What Kind of Sign?

All this is heady stuff. The new wine of the kingdom should not be drunk in isolation from the world, or we will lose touch with reality. To talk about the calling of the church is not to describe how things *are*, but how they *should* be. To announce the call of God is not enough – it must be followed by an act of discipleship. Yet we are continually reminded of the gap between dream and reality, between God's will and God's people. This is both because of the limitations of human existence and because of human sinfulness. Paul expresses this tension between confessing Jesus as Lord and living his Lordship:

> *'It is not ourselves that we proclaim; we proclaim Christ Jesus as Lord, and ourselves as your servants, for Jesus's sake. For the God who said "Out of darkness light shall shine", has caused his light to shine in our hearts, the light which is knowledge of the glory of God in the face of Jesus Christ. But we have only earthenware jars to hold this treasure, and this proves that such transcendent power does not come from us; it is God's alone.'* (2 Corinthians 4.5-7)

The importance of subjecting the church to the continual scrutiny of Scripture is so that it might never confuse the description of its calling with a description of 'the way things are'. Rhetoric is an important part of sharing a vision; poetry and metaphor are necessary ways of pushing language to its limits in order to point towards the vision of God's will. But we must distinguish between what the church *is* and what the church *ought* to be.

What kind of sign is the church? Not what kind of sign *ought* the church to be, what kind of sign *is* it, in fact? Perhaps we ought to speak of the church as a *counter-sign* of the kingdom, a counter-sign of the Lordship of Christ. Perhaps we should identify the church as an obstruction which repels people rather than attracts them, a stumbling block not because it faithfully lives out the foolishness of the gospel but because it does not. It is easy to attack the church for being unfaithful to its Lord, but it is also easy to come to terms with the failure in such a way as to accept it and institutionalize it.

It could be argued that denominations, as they currently exist, do just that. They accept the status quo, they exist and perpetuate themselves as though the divisions of the past were acceptable. They live as though to be divided was a normal state of affairs, rather than seeing division as the human reality which falls short of the divine vision. We must not confuse the way things are and the way things ought to be; nor should we accept the gap between them. Discipleship is about bridging the gap between vision and reality, and the promise of the Spirit is the promise of power to make that possible.

Vision and Hope

We saw how the vision of Israel's return to the promised land offered by the prophet of the exile was far above the actual events which fulfilled that vision.

The prophet was preaching to a dispirited people who had had their vision of being the people of God knocked out of them by the trauma of Jerusalem's destruction and the ambiguities of exile. They needed their sights raised, and so the propaganda language of the prophet was in itself a means of grace. It provided a vision of God which enabled some of the exiles to regain a vision of God's purpose for them and which, in turn, gave them back their identity as the people of God. This recovering of their own identity was a necessary stage which had to be undertaken before there could be a return to the promised land. The prophet's emphasis on the Lordship of God was an important basis for the regaining of a vision and that vision was an important factor in enabling some to respond to God's call when it came.

Here is a pattern we would do well to remember. Our hopes are based on God. The church is the Easter people because Easter shows us the God we are dealing with. It identifies him as the Father of Jesus Christ, the God who offers hope to the world because he did not abandon his Son to the tomb. At the same time, he offers hope to the world because in raising *Jesus* from death God shows that the gracious love we see in this Jesus is the very character of God.

This is the meaning of belief in the second coming of Christ at the end of the age. It expresses the conviction that the God we will face at the end of time is the God who has already come to us in Jesus. The love and forgiveness, the liberation and healing which we have found in him, will again be found in the God of the end.

The forgiveness of God is what keeps vision and reality in touch with each other. It is his forgiveness which first liberates us from sin and summons us to reach out in the baptismal path of loving discipleship. It is his forgiveness which enables us to face the stark reality of our continual sinfulness and failure. This forgiveness does not ignore reality, but empowers us to face it and sets us free to live out the vision despite our past. Visions are important, not as rods to strike us with, but as invitations of hope and love to draw us onward. Visions encourage us to reach out, to transcend the problems of the real world, not to ignore them.

This sharing of a vision is a vital part of being the church, and so the sharing of the ecumenical vision is important in calling the church to become her true self. Here is one account of the ecumenical vision. It sees the vision for the church in the larger context of a vision for humanity:

> 'The unity of the church and the renewal of human community are thus insep-
> arably linked not as two separate entities but as two concentric circles around
> the one, unique and the same pivotal event in history: God redeeming brokenness
> and bringing back into his communion 'all things' in order to renew them.' [17]

This is not a programme to be implemented but a vision to be shared. This hope is not something to end the struggling but is a hope which invites us to reach out and strive for it. Hope becomes life-giving because it shows us life and invites us to participate in that life.

> ' . . . in the medium of hope our theological concepts become not judgements which nail reality down to what it is, but anticipations which show reality its prospects and its future possibilities. Theological concepts do not give a fixed form to reality . . . they do not limp after reality . . . but they illuminate reality by displaying its future.' [18]

In this way we can talk about the ecumenical vision as the future of the church. In our biblical reflections we shall try to justify the claim that the unity of the church is the revealed will of God. But that will not specify the form of that unity or the way it is to be achieved. To claim that unity is the will of God is to use vision as a means of grace, to use hope as a creative and redemptive summons. Hope is therefore never a plain statement, but always an indictment of how things are and an invitation to participate in how things might be.

Therefore, a concern for a reconciled OIKOUMENE offers a vision which sees the variety of humanity reconciled within the church. There are black and white, female and male, poor and rich, young and old, within the reconciled community. Theological insight and cultural diversity enrich a community united in Christ. And this is just a foretaste of what is in store for all creation.

Here is the song of creation, where the creator God is also the redeemer who works a new creation. The hymns of the church are not private devotion to a secret deity but praises offered on behalf of all creation to the Lord of the Ages. Everything in the life of the church is offered for the world, the OIKOUMENE – its worship, its prayer, its sacraments, its service and witness. This is what it means to talk of the church as a priestly people. Worship is worship of God, but it is offered on behalf of all.

Yet, just as the Israelites needed to be called in the first place and then continually called to live up to their calling, so the church needs to be continually faced with this vision.

There are often people who will claim that unity is an unachieveable goal and that therefore it should not be sought. This is a counsel of despair. If we applied this to the life of the individual Christian, we would end up claiming that, because perfection is unattainable, the Christian doesn't need to try. 'Just accept the way things are and do not worry. God will forgive you.' It was just such an argument which Paul attacked at Rome when he wrote,

> 'What are we to say, then? Shall we persist in sin, so that there may be all the more grace? Certainly not! We died to sin: how can we live in it any longer? Have you forgotten that when we were baptized into union with Christ Jesus we were baptized into his death? By that baptism into his death we were buried with him, in order that, as Christ was raised from the dead by the glorious power of the Father, so also we might set out on a new life.' (Romans 6.1-4)

This is also true for the church. As the Easter people we gain our identity through living, as well as confessing, the lordship of Christ. To say that we will fail before we have begun is to fail in faith and in hope. The ultimate failure of faith it not to doubt along the way, or to stumble on the path. The ultimate failure of faith is to doubt the value of the journey. Visions are needed to invite us to share the journey, to encourage us on the journey and to provide us with directions along the way.

> 'Sometimes we are almost overcome by the smallness and insignificance of our lives; then we feel helpless. But as we feed upon the bread of life in worship we know again and again God's saving act in Christ in our own lives. We are astounded and surprised that the eternal purpose of God is persistently entrusted to ordinary people. That is the risk God takes. The forces of death are strong. The gift of life in Christ is stronger. We commit ourselves to live that life, with all its risks and joys, and therefore dare to cry, with all the host of heaven: "O death, where is your victory?" Christ is risen. He is risen indeed.'[19]

Notes

1. For a detailed historical survey of the word 'ecumenical' see W.A. Visser 't Hooft, 'The Meaning of Ecumenical', (London) 1953.

2. OIKOUMENE is the present passive participle of the verb OIKEO, to inhabit. It can therefore be translated into English as 'that which is inhabited' or 'the whole inhabited earth'.

3. See chapter 5.

4. For histories see R.E. Davies, 'The church in our Times: An Ecumenical History from a British Perspective' (London) 1979; J. Matthews, 'The Unity Scene' (London) 1986; and the larger 'official' history – ed. R. Rouse and S.C. Neill, 'A History of the Ecumenical Movement vol 1, 1517-1948' 3rd Ed (Geneva) 1986 and ed. H.E. Fey, 'The Ecumenical Advance – A History of the Ecumenical Movement vol 2. 1948-1968' 2nd Ed (Geneva) 1986.

5. 'The Churches survey their Task: the Report of the Conference at Oxford, July 1937, on Church, Community, and State', (London) pp168f.

6. D. Gill, 'Gathered for Life: Official Report, Sixth Assembly of the World Council of Churches' (Geneva and Grand Rapids) 1983 p197.

7. N. Goodall, 'The Uppsala Report' (Geneva) 1968 p223.

8. M. Kinnamon, 'Towards Visible Unity' (Geneva) 1982 p226.

9. Quoted in J. Bluck, 'Everyday Ecumenism: Can you take the World church home?' (Geneva) 1987 p4.

10. See chapter 3.

11. The classic text is J. Moltmann, 'Theology of Hope' ET (London) 1967,

but see also the report on the 1979 meeting of the Faith and Order Commission in Bangalore, 'Sharing in One Hope' (Geneva) 1978 and 'The Ecumenical Review, XXXX, 1 January 1979 pp5-50.

12. Hymn for Easter Sunday Vespers, quoted by A. Papaderos in his essay 'Ecumenism as Celebration' in P. Webb, 'Faith and Faithfulness: Essays on Contemporary Ecumenical Themes, A tribute to Philip A. Potter' (Geneva) 1984 p28.

13. Pope John Paul II.

14. See chapter 7.

15. An example of the way in which baptism has been seen to be undergirded by the Lordship of Christ is the way in which it has been related to martyrdom. When, during persecution, new converts have been martyred before being baptized, their very martyrdom has been described as a baptism. If baptism expresses a willingness to make Christ Lord of my life, then martyrdom is a supreme offering of that life. This understanding was helped by such passages as Mark 10.38-39, where drinking the cup and being baptized may be seen as referring to the cross.

16. The first form of the People's Acclamation from 'New Orders for the Mass in India' published by the National Biblical Catechetical and Liturgical Centre, Bangalore (1974) and printed in M. Thurian and G. Wainwright, 'Baptism and Eucharist: Ecumenical Convergence in Celebration' (Geneva and Grand Rapids) 1983 p189.

17. N.A. Nissiotis in G. Limouris, 'Church, Kingdom, World: The Church as Mystery and Prophetic Sign' (Geneva) 1986 p157.

18. J. Moltmann, 'Theology of Hope' pp35-36.

19. The closing words from the message from the Vancouver assembly in 1983 printed in D. Gill, 'Gathered for Life: Official Report, Sixth Assembly of the World Council of Churches' (Geneva and Grand Rapids) 1983 p3-4.

Chapter Three

BIBLICAL REFLECTIONS
AND THE WILL OF GOD

At the heart of this book is the conviction that the search for unity in the church and in the world is *biblical*. However, we need to clarify what we mean by this claim, and to ask how it is to be tested and what its implications might be for the ecumenical quest.

It is not the purpose of this chapter to develop a 'Biblical Doctrine of Unity', even if such a task were possible. Neither is this an attempt at detailed exegesis of particular passages. In fact, it has been partly a frustration at the way in which arguments for ecumenism have frequently revolved around a small number of texts (eg. John 17, 1 Corinthians 1 and Ephesians 4) that has led to the present work. These 'classic' passages cannot be ignored, but we must attempt to look for an overall pattern, rather than simply pick out a few purple passages which meet the needs of the moment.

Because the claim is being made that unity is a theme which runs through the Bible, [1] the approach here will be a thematic one. There are, of course, dangers in approaching the Bible this way. For example there is the difficulty of selecting material and the danger of the use and misuse of passages to fit a supposed pattern. Nonetheless, such a thematic approach is necessary if we are to test our project against the main 'drift' of scripture. If we can provide evidence to suggest that the concern for unity is a substantial concern of the biblical material, then we will have a challenge for today's church. As a result, the arguments of the following chapters will be strengthened by this testing of our theme 'under the Word'.

Concern for Peace

We begin our survey of themes with the concern for peace. Because the divisions of the church are an inheritance of bitterness and because the divisions of the denominations often keep people apart, we can claim that the yearning for peace is a legitimate part of the search for unity.

The understanding of peace which we find in the Old Testament is a broad one which provides a framework for understanding a variety of ideas. The Hebrew word *shalom* is usually translated *peace*, but it is important to realize that it means more than *the absence of war*. It has the wider, positive meaning of *well-being* and *wholeness* which is anyway, we may reflect, a necessary component in the avoidance of war. Shalom has been described as 'the harmony of a caring community informed at every point by its awareness of God'.[2] This sense of harmony can refer to the relations between states (1 Kings 5.4) or between individuals (Zechariah 6.13). While shalom is very much concerned with material well-being, it is at the same time, seen as a gift from God who is described by Gideon as 'Yahweh-Shalom' (Judges 6.24).

A number of the prophets struggled against those whom they saw as false prophets who had offered the people that promise of peace which they had wanted to hear (eg. Micah 3.5-11, Jeremiah 23.16-24 and Ezekiel 13.1-16). The issue was not that there was no message of peace to proclaim. But the false prophets disregarded the sins of the people and called an absence of hostilities 'peace', ignoring the injustice which distorted the community from within and the political instability which threatened it from without. The Old Testament prophets rejected such a superficial peace because they believed that God's will is for shalom – wholeness, righteousness and justice. Because such a view of peace is, in its fulness, beyond the normal human experience, shalom eventually became a part of that future hope which the prophets promised and for which humanity yearns. Such a hope of shalom was so radically different from the circumstances within which the prophets proclaimed their oracles, that this shalom was envisaged as a result of God's special, saving action – and so the long-awaited Messiah was linked to the hope of shalom (eg. Isaiah 9.6-7).

Nowhere in the Old Testament does shalom seem to denote a specifically inward peace – its meaning is social, referring not to emotions so much as to relationships. As such, it provides a framework of expectation about God's concern for the wholeness of community life, for right dealing between persons and nations, about reconciliation between groups and individuals. Underneath all this is an awareness that peace with each other is linked with God's grace as well as our response.

In the New Testament, the Greek word *eirene* covers a range of meanings from simple greetings to the hope of salvation. When Paul pleads with the Corinthians to have order in their charismatic worship, he bases his plea on the nature of God and his will for the world: 'For God is not a God of disorder but of peace' (1 Corinthians 14.33). When the birth of the Messiah is announced by the angels (Luke 2.1-14), when the gospel is described as 'the gospel of peace' (Ephesians 6.15) and when Christians are called to live in peace with everyone (Hebrews 12.14), these affirmations and hopes are based on the centrality of peace in the nature and purposes of God – for God is 'the God of peace' (1 Thessalonians 5.23).

Peace with God and peace with each other are linked (Ephesians 2.14.22 and Romans 14.17). Jesus challenged the man who was not at peace with his neighbour to sort out that relationship before seeking peace with God at the altar (Matthew 5.23-24). In Matthew 5.9 the peacemakers are pronounced 'blessed', for God calls them his children – in promoting the healing of relationships they are like him. We see this in its fullness in the person and work of Jesus Christ who, in Colossians 1.20 is said 'to reconcile all things, whether on earth or heaven'. Here we have a cosmic shalom.

If we are to explore the development of *shalom* in the New Testament, we need to extend this survey beyond the word *eirene*. In the Old Testament, the ordering of the community of Israel, through the law, and the quality of life of the people of God, was seen as a part of God's purposes for all peoples. When the future peace is anticipated in the vision of the gathering of the nations at Mount Zion (Isaiah 2.2-4 and Micah 4.1-4), we again see the link between the vocation of the people of God and the divine plan for creation. Without making any claims as to the causal link between these ideas, we can see a parallel between these concerns and the idea of fellowship *(koinonia)* in the New Testament.

The group of related Greek words which are translated as *fellowship* move around the ideas of 'partnership' or 'having things in common'. The inner communion with Christ by faith, expressed in the Lord's Supper, is a communion shared with others. There is a bond between those who belong to Christ and this manifests itself in a concern for the fellowship. The Pauline greeting, 'The grace of the Lord Jesus Christ, and the love of God, and the fellowship of the Holy Spirit, be with you all', (2 Corinthians 13.14), is a text frequently used in worship and Christian meetings today. In 1 John 1.3-7, the fellowship which believers have with each other is possible because of participation in the fellowship of the Father and the Son. Although these two writers express themselves in different ways, they both point to the experience of oneness achieved through the activity of God.

A striking use of the idea of fellowship is that of material sharing (Acts 2.42). The collection of money amongst Gentile churches for the impoverished church in Jerusalem is seen as an act of service which follows in the example of Christ and is an expression of fellowship (Romans 15.26 and 2 Corinthians 8.4). While this fellowship speaks of the relationship between believers within the gathered church, there is a parallel with Israel's concern for her community life. In so far as Israel and the church are to be seen as instruments in the purposes of God, we can argue that this shalom, or peace, or fellowship, is an anticipation and sign of that which God plans for the whole cosmos.

Some implications of our survey ought already to be clear. In identifying a concern for peace for the people of God and, ultimately, for the whole universe, we have identified a theme which is close to that of unity. This does not mean that the two ideas are identified as the same thing, but they are inextricably linked.

We have seen how shalom is not a superficial cessation of hostilities, or an uneasy co-existence. It is about wholeness of relationships, based on mutual trust and support. It is *between* individuals and groups, so it presupposes the kind of community where there will be responsible freedom and variety, expressed in harmony. At this stage we must not use a definition of shalom to give specific content to the unity which is still ahead of us, but we should, nonetheless, note some lessons along the way.

Here is more than co-existence. Here is peace wrought by the sacrifice of Christ. Here is fellowship which has a material expression and a peace which has communal concerns. Here is a wholeness for the people of God which is granted us as 'a foretaste of the heavenly banquet prepared for all mankind'.

A number of biblical themes overlap, as different pictures express the same reality from different angles. We could explore the links between shalom and the Kingdom of God, especially in its embodiment in the mission of Jesus. To do so would be to present a corporate vision of reality in its relationship to God which is centred in Jesus Christ – in his teaching and actions, death and resurrection. But the theme of the Kingdom will be pursued later, in chapter 7. Here, we need to note how, even without explicit reference to the word 'peace', the theme of shalom can be seen at the heart of the New Testament. Not only that, but the Kingdom is a theme which makes demands on the followers of Jesus, raising questions of discipleship and faithfulness.

The Ministry of Reconciliation

Although not a major emphasis for other biblical writers, the theme of *reconciliation* is a central one for Paul. [3] Its very centrality is important in our attempt to establish a pattern of ideas around the theme of unity flowing out of the gospel itself. To demonstrate the importance of this theme for Paul, we can note the assessment of T.W. Manson:

> **'Reconciliation** is thus the key word of Paul's Gospel so far as its working out in Christ is concerned. The driving force behind the Gospel is the love of God. The **modus operandi** is reconciliation.' [4]

R.P. Martin claims that reconciliation is 'the chief theme or "centre" of his missionary and pastoral thought and practice'. [5] He goes on to demonstrate how the theme of reconcilation is not a Pauline invention which stands over and against the teaching of Jesus, but rather something which grows out of important aspects of Jesus' witness and ministry. The concern of Jesus for outcasts and sinners, the fight against evil in the proclamation of the Kingdom of God, the declaration of God's parenthood and the invitation to his followers to be children of God, may together be seen as the source from which Paul's stream of preaching on reconciliation flows. [5]

Paul uses the idea of reconciliation as a way of talking about what God has achieved through the death and resurrection of Jesus Christ. There are three important facets to his use of this theme; two of them can be found in the passage 2 Corinthians 5.18-20:

'All this has been the work of God. He has reconciled us to himself through Christ, and has enlisted us in this service of reconciliation. God was in Christ reconciling the world to himself, no longer holding people's misdeeds against them, and has entrusted us with the message of reconciliation. We are therefore Christ's ambassadors. It is as if God were appealing to you through us: we implore you in Christ's name, be reconciled to God!'

The first point is this: sinful humanity is reconciled to God and this is good news. Alongside other pictures, such as justification and victory, Paul uses the picture of a healed relationship. This is no easy dismissal of differences, for it is wrought at the cost of the cross (Romans 5.11). However, the emphasis in the talk of reconciliation is not on *how* the forgiveness has been achieved, but on the good news that it *is* so. We could say that the emphasis on reconciliation language is on the new shalom that is made possible in Christ. The root of the word for reconciliation has the meaning of 'change' and we can see how Paul proclaims the good news as a transformed relationship between God and humanity. Indeed, the language is wider than that, for there is the hint of a new world through the reconciliation of all things in Christ:

'For anyone united to Christ, there is a new creation; the old order has gone; a new order has already begun'. (2 Corinthians 5.17)

'For in him (Christ) God in all his fullness chose to dwell, and through him to reconcile all things to himself, making peace through the shedding of his blood on the cross – all things, whether on earth or in heaven.' (Colossians 1.19-20)

So the purposes of God, achieved through the violence and agony of a sacrificial death, are the healing of his relationships with humanity, and, ultimately, the healing of a creation which has been distorted by sin, as the biblical story of the Fall testifies.

Secondly, 2 Corinthians 5.18-20 proclaims that those who have been reconciled to God are in turn entrusted with participation in the service of reconciling others to God. [6] Here is a rolling programme of reconciliation, reminiscent of Jesus' teaching on forgiveness, where those who have been forgiven are called to forgive others (Matthew 18.23-35). This is a common theme of Paul where he exhorts those who have received salvation to preach the good news to those still without hope. Indeed, Eduard Schweitzer has commented that, 'Paul never speaks of his conversion, but only of his calling'. [7]

With the existentialist influences of Twentieth Century thought, and the catastrophic wars in our age, reconciliation has been a recurring theme in the proclamation and thought of the church of our time. We cannot underestimate the importance of this aspect of Paul's presentation of the gospel for a world broken and endangered by strife. Those who receive the benefits of God's reconciling action in Christ, are called, as part of that action, to participate in the ministry of reconciliation. Thus the challenge to a divided church is made in terms which cannot easily be ignored. But this claim brings us to the third dimension of Paul's use of the theme of reconciliation.

The transformation which comes about, as a result of being reconciled to God, means that those reconciled to him are also reconciled to each other. Those in the church at Ephesus who were Gentile converts to Christianity are reminded that, formerly, they were outside God's covenant and strangers to the community of Israel.

'Once you were far off, but now in union with Christ Jesus you have been brought near through the shedding of Christ's blood. For he is himself our peace. Gentiles and Jews, he has made the two one, and in his own body of flesh and blood has broken down the barrier of enmity which separated them; for he annulled the law with its rules and regulations, so as to create out of the two a single humanity in himself, thereby making peace. This was his purpose, to reconcile the two in a single body to God through the cross, by which he killed the enmity.' (Ephesians 2.13-16)

Later in the epistle, the Ephesians are exhorted to 'Spare no effort to make fast with bonds of peace the unity which the Spirit gives'. (Ephesians 4.3) As with other themes, so with reconciliation, Paul announces something to be the case and then exhorts his readers to make this announcement a living reality. His graphic description of a dividing wall between Jew and Gentile has been variously interpreted[8], but its main point is clear. The God who reconciles people to himself also establishes a new relationship which transforms their relationship with each other. In dealing with the sin which separates us from God, he is dealing with the same sin which separates us from each other.

Paul proclaims this message by applying it to other divisions in his letter to the Galatians:

'It is through faith that you are all sons of God in union with Christ Jesus. Baptized into union with him, you have all put on Christ like a garment. There is no such thing as Jew and Greek, slave and freeman, male and female; for you are all one person in Christ Jesus'. (Galatians 3.26-28)

Paul has been using the picture of inheritance as a means of describing how believers will receive the blessings of salvation. That is why he is concerned to describe all Christians as 'sons', for in Roman law it was the male children who inherited. But this is a common inheritance where all are 'sons' and all have put on Christ and divisions are removed. In the light of Paul's teaching elsewhere, perhaps we should say that distinctions remain in their rich variety within the Christian community, but those distinctions are not the basis of division or enmity.

Here again is a challenge for the church. If our relationships with each other are changed by the same action of God in Christ which has reconciled us to him, then the worship and life which celebrates our salvation ought also to celebrate our changed relationships with each other. This claim inevitably involves an ecclesiology, an understanding of the nature of the church, but we must note that its place in the argument arises out of an exposition of the gospel of salvation – which all our churches would claim to have in common.

There is not sufficient space to undertake a comprehensive study of the church in the New Testament, but we shall need to explore the idea of *unity* in the church. This is not only because of its obvious relevance to our argument as a whole, but because it flows naturally from what we have discovered about the themes of peace and reconciliation, and also because it flows naturally into an examination of the theme of love.

Unity in the Church

In exploring the theme of reconciliation we have seen how the Ephesians were told in 2.14, 'Gentiles and Jews, he has made the two one'. Inevitably, the theme of reconciliation leads to the theme of unity. If reconciliation is the *act* of bringing together those who are divided, or at enmity with each other, then unity is the *result* of that action. *The gospel of reconciliation* leads to the bringing together of God and humanity. A *ministry of reconciliation* leads to the sharing in the mission of God 'namely, that the universe, everything in heaven and on earth, might be brought into a unity in Christ' (Ephesians 1.10). Reconciliation with God leads to reconciliation with each other and that in turn leads to unity in the church.

An illustration of the gospel of reconciliation leading to unity in Christ is found in Acts chapter 2 where Luke tells of the gift of the Spirit at Pentecost. Those Jews who had come to Jerusalem for the festival from different parts of the ancient world are said to understand the apostles' preaching in their various native languages. It has been argued that Luke presents us with a symbolic reversal of the story of Babel. In Genesis 11 human pride and ambition lead to an attempt to scale heaven by means of a tower. In the ancient story the attempt is foiled by God dispersing the people throughout the earth and giving them different languages so that they cannot organize such a titanic assault again. In Genesis, language is identified as a symbol of human division [9]; in turn, the crowd's understanding of the apostles' preaching becomes a symbol of division overcome. This sets the scene for Luke's story of the spread of the gospel through the ancient world until it reached the centre in Rome. He affirms that *all* may hear and respond to the good news of Jesus Christ and that the Spirit, at work in the preaching and the coming to faith, is a Spirit who unites and heals broken humanity. This is focussed in his portrait of the early community in Jerusalem in 2.42:

'They met constantly to hear the apostles teach, and to share the common life, to break bread, and to pray.'

But unity is not only the goal of reconciliation. Unity is also that state of harmony which holds within itself the rich diversity of God's gifts. So in the fellowship of the church there is a shalom which does not make everyone the same but enables each to contribute 'a special gift, a particular share in the bounty of Christ' (Ephesians 4.7). In Romans 12.4-5 Paul writes,

'For just as in a single human body there are many limbs and organs, all with different functions, so we who are united with Christ, though many, form one body, and belong to one another as its limbs and organs.'

The picture of the human body is a rich image of diversity in unity and was probably not original to Paul. [10] But its emphasis is on the variety of gifts which need to be exercised within a local congregation. It is offered in passing as Paul proceeds to describe some of the gifts and encourages their use in mutual service.

His use of the image in 1 Corinthians 12 is less eirenic, for he is writing to a church threatened with splits and factions. These factions seem to have been aggravated by a pride in the 'gifts of the Spirit', especially the gift of speaking in tongues. The picture is of a young, enthusiastic congregation whose members are intent on their individual accomplishments rather than the loving spirit of Christ. Paul's emphasis here is on the unity of which the diversity is an enriching aspect:

'Christ is like a single body with its many limbs and organs, which, many as they are, together make up one body; for in the one Spirit we were all brought into one body by baptism, whether Jews or Greeks, slaves or free, we were all given that one Spirit to drink.' *(1 Corinthians 12.12-13)*

After explaining that all these gifts are put in perspective by the exercising of a Christ-like love, he continues his instructions on how the local community is to use these various gifts: 'To sum up, my friends . . . see that all aim to build up the church' (1 Corinthians 14.26). The diversity of gifts could be seen as a reconciliation from within – the building up of the community by the reconciling Spirit who bestows these various gifts on the church.

When earlier he has spoken of the Lord's Supper he has expounded it as a sacrament of unity:

'When we bless the cup of blessing, is it not a means of sharing in the blood of Christ? When we break bread, is it not a means of sharing in the body of Christ? Because there is one loaf, we, though many, are one body; for it is one loaf of which we all partake.' *(1 Corinthians 10.16-17)*

Here the eucharistic meal is an expression of the unity of the community. Just as the community is a group of disparate individuals and groups who have been reconciled by Christ, so their sharing of the one loaf is a testimony to the one Lord in whom they themselves are one.

To be One

In the letter to the Ephesians the imagery is turned around. Whereas in 1 Corinthians the Spirit bestows the diverse gifts, in Ephesians the gift of the Spirit is the unity of the church and the various gifts are the bounty of Christ. Unity is presented as a quality or state of the church which is given by the Spirit but which still needs to be secured by the Christ-like behaviour of the members:

> 'Spare no effort to make fast with bonds of peace the unity which the Spirit gives. There is one body and one Spirit, just as there is also one hope held out in God's call to you; one Lord, one faith, one baptism; one God and Father of all, who is over all and through all and in all.' (Ephesians 4.3-6)

In these verses we may note that the word 'one' appears seven times and the word 'all' four times. This confession of the life of the church is entwined with a Trinitarian description of God and his purposes. The body (the church) is created by the activity of the Spirit who summons us in hope. The life of this community is centred on the one Lord Jesus Christ in whom we trust and with whom we are united in baptism. All is founded on and surrounded with and penetrated by the Father who, as creator, is in, over and through all. In each case we are told of one Spirit, one Lord and one Father. So the unity of God is the reason for and the means by which we may speak of, and hope for, the unity of the church.

> 'God's oneness is directly, ie. causatively, dynamically, effectively . . . related to the unity of the church. Because God is one, his people are one and are to live on the basis and in the recognition of unity.' [11]

This oneness which links the life of the church to the life of God is a theme which we can also find in the Gospel of John. It has even been argued by one scholar that this is the main theme of the whole Fourth Gospel. [12] At three significant points the theme of 'oneness' emerges and links the relationship of unity between Jesus and the Father with the relationship between Jesus and those who believe in him and the relationship his followers have with one another. 'Oneness' is clearly not a mathematical term but a word which expresses a relationship between two distinct but united parties. Thus Jesus says:

> 'I am the good shepherd; I know my own and my own know me, as the Father knows me and I know the Father; and I lay down my life for the sheep. But there are other sheep of mine, not belonging to this fold; I must lead them as well, and they too will listen to my voice. There will then be one flock, one shepherd.' (John 10.14-16)

There will be one flock, transcending national and any other boundaries we try to draw. The basis of this oneness is the one shepherd, Jesus himself. It is his death which conclusively reveals him to be such a shepherd, able to gather the scattered into one flock, for the good shepherd is identified as the one who does not run away but lays down his life for the sheep (verse 11).

This theme of gathering a scattered flock appears again in chapter 11. John reports with heavy theological irony the judgement of Caiaphas, the high priest, that it is expedient that one man die for the people, rather than the nation be destroyed. There follows a verse of explanation which reveals the importance of the oneness theme for the evangelist:

> '. . . and not for the nation only, but to gather into one the children of God who are scattered abroad.' (John 11.52 RSV)

Here we discover the church to be a gathering of the children of God, from all kinds of geographical locations, whose gathering is made possible by the death of Jesus. How the cross achieves this is not explained, but its goal is the oneness of those who at present are scattered. Here is a future hope which has as its basis God's action in Christ. We can compare this with Paul's presentation of the work of Christ as the gospel of reconciliation and also with the words of Jesus in John 12.32 which have an even broader compass:

> 'And when I am lifted up from the earth I shall draw everyone to myself.'

However, the theme of oneness in the Fourth Gospel reaches its climax in chapter 17, sometimes called 'the high priestly prayer' or 'the departing prayer of Jesus', when he prays for his disciples and for those who are not yet his disciples, but will one day put their faith in him:

> 'May they all be one; as you, Father, are in me, and I in you, so also may they be in us, that the world may believe that you sent me. The glory which you gave me I have given to them, that they may be one, as we are one; I in them and you in me, may they be perfectly one. Then the world will know that you sent me, and that you loved them as you loved me.' (John 17.21-23)

The oneness of Father and Son is not explained but is simply stated and offered as the basis for the prayer and hope of the chapter. Jesus prays for the unity of the church but not for his relationship with the Father. That unity is taken for granted, yet in itself it provides a pointer as to the nature of the unity sought for the church.

> 'The Father remains the Father and the Son remains the Son . . . Oneness in John does not mean the erasure of differences.' [13]

It is clear, both from the distinctiveness of the Father from the Son and from the prayer that the Son and his followers will be one, that this oneness includes differentiation. Just as here we have no mystical assimilation, so the oneness of the followers may, by analogy, be seen to be a oneness of harmony rather than unison! Yet we must be careful about building too strong a claim for diversity from this passage. The unity is the oneness of those who put their faith in Jesus. *He* is the basis of their unity: their oneness with him, and through him with the Father, is the basis of their oneness with each other. [14] We must not use the distinctiveness of Father and Son, and therefore the diversity of believers, as the beginning of a defence of division. That would be to devalue the oneness which is, after all, the keynote of the passage. The oneness is visible because it enables the world to recognise Jesus. Here is not a justification of division but a challenge to explore the meaning of unity. [15]

The purpose of this unity is clearly linked to mission. Just as the oneness of Jesus with the Father is expressed by his being sent into the world, so the oneness of his followers will testify to who Jesus is — he who is one with the Father. Thus the life of the church is called to be a clear sign pointing to Jesus — the unity of his followers will point towards the identification of Jesus with the Father. The credibility of the claim that God confronts us in this Jesus is to be tested by what his coming has achieved in the corporate life of his followers (verse 23).

We must not read into the Fourth Gospel, or the letter to the Ephesians, the theological ideas of later Trinitarian debate. However, these passages do testify to the rich diversity of the biblical experience of God which was later to lead to the development of that doctrine. In Ephesians 4.3-6 we may note the repeated emphasis on 'one', like a drum beat (or heart beat?), and the way in which the diversity of God's activity enables the church to be caught up in its life-giving patterns.

While that passage speaks of 'Spirit', 'Lord' and 'Father' as each in turn impinges on the church and the world, there is not yet that circularity of divine relationship which was to mark the later developments of the doctrine. However, the way in which the earthly body of believers is caught up into the varied divine activity leads us on to explore another biblical beginning which was eventually to be fed into the developing doctrine of the Trinity. This is the theme of God's love and our participation in its dynamic and sacrificial movement.

The Love of Christ Leaves us No Choice
While we do not want to underestimate the diversity of theologies in the New Testament, there are themes which recur; *love* is a good example of a theme which pulls together various testimonies. This in itself might give us cause to hope that in love we may find an integrating factor for contemporary Christianity. Up to a point this is true, but we must not lose sight of the differing treatments of love by the different authors.

Nor should we lose sight of the liberating, yet limiting, quality of love itself.

The very concern with love-in-action (the emphasis not just on love-of-humanity or love-of-God, but love-of-neighbour), means that love always has to find concrete expression. This means its incarnation will vary from place to place. Love is so much more than a principle that we cannot even ask about love-of-neighbour. We have to be even more specific and ask about our love-of-THIS-neighbour. Yet while the theme of love will not provide us with a programme for union, it will offer a basis for our endeavours and a Christ-centred quality for our relationships.

> 'My dear friends, let us love one another, because the source of love is God. Everyone who loves is a child of God and knows God, but the unloving know nothing of God, for God is love. This is how he showed his love among us: he sent his only Son into the world that we might have life through him.' (1 John 4.7-10)

One of the reasons why love pervades the New Testament is that it provides a framework for understanding the activity of God in the past of the Old Testament, in Jesus, in the life of the believer and in the future. Creation and redemption are the outworking of the love of God. Although Paul's letter to the Romans is usually seen as 'the epistle of faith', it would be well for us to note that the climax of his exposition of the gospel is the affirmation that there is 'nothing in all creation that can separate us from the love of God in Christ Jesus our Lord' (Romans 8.39). Similarly, the second half of the letter concludes with practical ethical exhortations based on love and the whole letter ends with greetings: 'Greet one another with the kiss of peace. All Christ's churches send you their greetings' (Romans 16.16).

These ethical exhortations provide a continuity between the teaching of Paul and the teaching of Jesus. In the synoptic gospels Jesus responds to the question 'Which commandment is first of all?' with the response:

> 'The first is, "Hear, O Israel: the Lord our God is the one Lord, and you must love the Lord your God with all your heart, with all your soul, with all your mind, and with all your strength". The second is this: "Love your neighbour as yourself". No other commandment is greater than these.' (Mark 12.29-31)

In the teaching of Jesus there are three dimensions to this love. We are called to love God, to love our neighbour and to love our neighbour even when he is our enemy. This radical command goes beyond the Old Testament law and transforms our understanding of human relationships.

But the coming of Jesus does not only mean a new commandment, it also means a new situation. Jesus is the one who comes announcing the forgiveness of sins (Mark 2.1-12). His eating with the outcasts of society, his parable of the non-forgiving debtor and his parables of the lost sheep, coin and sons all demonstrate the way in which the coming of Jesus in gracious and forgiving love has changed everything (Mark 2.15-17, Matthew 18.23-35 and

Luke 15.1-32). The very nature of this new situation, because it is about divine forgiveness as well as the announcing of a new way, means that it is a revelation of God. So the teaching and actions of Jesus, and ultimately his death (Mark 10.45), become a proclamation of the nature of God, whose nature is revealed in his saving action in Jesus.

For Paul this saving action is focussed in the cross:

> 'For the love of Christ controls us once we have reached the conclusion that one man died for all and therefore all mankind has died. He died for all so that those who live should cease to live for themselves, and should live for him who for their sake died and was raised to life . . . For anyone united to Christ, there is a new creation; the old order has gone; a new order has already begun.' (2 Corinthians 5.14-15,17)

Here is the appeal of God through the loving sacrifice of Christ, an appeal which calls for an answering love. Thus the Spirit enables us to respond to the love we see in Christ: 'through the Holy Spirit he has given us, God's love has flooded our hearts' (Romans 5.5).

For Paul the love of God is not only to be found in the appeal of the crucified Lord. The divine love is at work in the Old Testament (Romans 9.25) and now, through all that God has done in Christ and continues to do through his Spirit, there is nothing which can separate us from his love.

Paul believes that it is God's purpose to create a new humanity and so the response of love is to be seen as part of the new creation. The loving God calls us in freedom to work out our 'own salvation in fear and trembling' (Philippians 2.12), yet the direction is clear: 'the only thing that counts is faith expressing itself through love' (Galatians 5.6).

It is in the wonderful passage on love in 1 Corinthians 13 that we most clearly glimpse the centrality of love for Paul. Amidst his discussion of the spiritual gifts which were causing factions and splits at Corinth, he talks about 'the best way of all'. Whatever insights of prophecy, or whatever actions of charity or martyrdom, are demonstrated by Christians, they are nothing unless there is love. Then, in presenting the triad of faith, hope and love he insists that the greatest of all is love. Here is the heart of it all — there will come a time when neither faith nor hope will be needed, but because love is of the nature of God and of the essence of the new humanity, there will always be love.

In the Johannine writings Jesus Christ is again portrayed as the revelation of God's love. Here the focus is on God's love of the world and this is echoed in the call to love each other:

> 'God so loved the world that he gave his only Son, that everyone who has faith in him may not perish but have eternal life.' (John 3.16)

'I give you a new commandment: love one another; as I have loved you, so you are to love one another.' (John 13.34)

The priority of love is made clear in the first epistle:

'We love because he loved us first. But if someone says "I love God", while at the same time hating his fellow-Christian, he is a liar. If he does not love the fellow-Christian whom he has seen, he is incapable of loving God whom he has not seen. We have this command from Christ himself: whoever loves God must love his fellow-Christian too.' (John 4.19-21)

This is very close to the concern of 1 Corinthians chapter 13, not only in the portrayal of love as the foundation of all Christian behaviour, but, in the grounding of this in the prior love of God. We see love as something rooted in the very nature and activity of God.

If we look again at the prayer of Jesus in John 17 we find the themes of love and unity brought together. The unity of the community is seen as a witness to the truth of the claims made about Jesus. The authority of the church's proclamation is brought into question by the disunity of believers. But more than this – the crucial test as to the divine origin of Jesus is whether or not those who follow him display love one to another. This love is seen as the same love as the Father has for the Son and the Son for the Father. In other words, the prayer is that the community might have the very love which is the love of God.

'It is not for these alone (his present disciples) that I pray, but for those also who through their words put their faith in me. May they all be one: as you, Father, are in me, and I in you, so also may they be in us, that the world may believe that you sent me.' (John 17.20-21)

As we have seen in our examination of the theme of *oneness*, this mutual in-dwelling is of the earthly Jesus with his heavenly Father: in this human-divine relationship of love we find a model for our own relationship with God.[14] Again the message is clear. We cannot separate our love of God from our love of each other.

This exposition of the theme of love still leaves a gap between its appeal and the way in which it is to be lived in the concrete situation of the church today. Nonetheless, there are markers which we cannot ignore. In particular, we cannot condone a form of church life which is satisfied with a relationship with God while despising or ignoring other Christians. The challenge for us is to decide how love must compel us to act. How can institutions love? The answer is that they cannot, but they can make loving easier or more difficult. So we are charged to scrutinize our structures in the light of the biblical call to participate in the love of God.

The Will of God?

Unity and peace are biblical themes which hold before us an affirmation of how things should be. They are based on the belief in one God, who holds together the diversity of creation as a harmonious whole. So the universe is seen as a reflection of the glory of God rather than the theatre of a cosmic, dualistic battle. But because this is an expression of faith and hope and because the world is divided and our human experience is of a disintegrated cosmos, the theme of redemption is presented, at least in part, as a message of reconciliation. Christ is crucified by the forces of enmity but he is raised to be the Lord of the church.

So we can claim that it is God's will that the new way be seen in the new people – a new creation of reconciled humanity. Because of this the holding together of unity and diversity in the church becomes a sign of hope for the universe. So Christians are called to *strive* for what is *given* – the love of God. Called to participate in the love of the Son for the Father, and of the Father for the Son, the church becomes the people of God because the world is able to identify the church with the Lord of the church.

Here is a challenge to the church to face the issue of unity not so much as a political or practical problem, but as the vocation of the people of God – a calling to be the Body of Christ, a people who display the loving of God.

It is always dangerous to invoke the will of God as a reason for doing something. It is easy to baptize one's prejudices with a self-righteous justification. But if we are to concern ourselves with individual or corporate discipleship, we cannot avoid wrestling with the question, 'What is the will of God?'

There will be two kinds of response to this question. On the one hand, there are the ultimate answers – affirmations of God's concern for the human project as a whole, together with grand statements about the nature of the church. This is the kind of response we have found through our enquiring into biblical themes. The themes are not wholly abstract because they have been developed in the specific historical situations of the biblical writers. But they need to be re-applied to our situation if they are to challenge us. They provide us with a direction, with concerns that bear the weight of divine will – concerns for peace, reconciliation, and unity in love.

The second kind of response still has to be undertaken. To some extent it is beyond the scope of this book – to examine the various detailed, tactical ways forward in the next steps towards unity. However, we will need to make a start if only to try and unpack what kind of unity we should be seeking.

Our *search* has begun. The *debate* must now develop by exploring the difference between *division* and *diversity* and by examining the possible foundations for mutual acceptance and unity. This will involve a study of the early years of the Christian church and its testimony within the Bible and then creeds. It will also involve a discussion of the kind of language we use when talking of God. This debate is in fact the next step in the search. If we are agreed that the Christian gospel impels us towards a search for unity, then we must examine both our disunity and the shape of our hope that things might be different.

Notes

1. Robert McAfee Brown claims that the impulse of the Bible is towards unity. 'The Ecumenical Revolution' (London) 1967.

2. J.V. Taylor, 'Enough is Enough' (London) 1975 p41.

3. See R.P. Martin, 'Reconciliation: A study of Paul's Theology' (London) 1981. On the controversial matter of whether or not Paul is the author of Ephesians and Colossians, this is not the place for a lengthy discussion of the critical issues. The use of the name Paul in the text does not assume Pauline authorship but is simply a verbal convenience indicating that the work was written by Paul or attributed to him.

4. T.W. Manson in M. Black (ed.), 'On Paul and Jesus' (London) 1963.

5. He writes, 'Reconciliation is more than a theological code-word for God's work of restoring men and women to himself. It marks the way of life to which those people are summoned by the fact that they are reconciled and share in God's continuing ministry of reconcilement in the world. The life of the Pauline congregations was for the apostle one of the most telling methods of evangelism since that corporate life was meant to reflect both the character of God and the outworking of the message as it applied to the human context. As Christians love one another, forgave and were compassionate to one another, it showed forth in their mutual attitudes that they shared a new spirit which was not self-centred, hard-hearted or spiteful but one that made for unity and harmony, so they were giving expression to the authenticity of the message of reconciliation.' 'Reconciliation: A Study in Paul's Theology' p230.

6. See also Colossians 1.22.

7. E. Schweitzer. 'The Letter to the Colossians' ET (London) 1982 p93.

8. eg. (i) the wall which separated the Court of the Gentiles from the rest of the Jerusalem temple (ii) the curtain which separated the Holy of Holies in the temple (iii) a spiritual fence around the law made as a safety margin by the scribes in their oral interpretation.

9. Today we may well see language as an example of rich cultural diversity but in Genesis 11 and Acts 2 we need to see it as a symbol of disunity. Probably the story of Babel originated as a myth to explain how different languages came to exist (a pre-biblical 'Just So Story') and it was then taken and used as a story to demonstrate the divisive nature of pride and ambition – perhaps reflecting the urban experience of the Hebrew exiles in Babylon. The point for us is that Luke uses the story to underline the universalism and reconciling power of the Spirit's activity.

10. The usual passage from antiquity which is quoted is the speech put by Livy (ii 32) into the mouth of Menenius Agrippa during the revolt of the plebs of Rome. See C.K. Barrett, 'The Epistle to the Romans' (London) 1957 p236.

11. M. Barth, 'Ephesians 4-6' (New York) 1974 p465.

12. See Mark L. Appold, 'The Oneness Motif in the Fourth Gospel' (Tubingen) 1976.

13. 'The Oneness Motif' p282.

14. R.E. Brown suggests that the emphasis on unity in the letter to the Ephesians, the Fourth Gospel and the letters to Timothy may be no accident. Arguing that they may well be roughly contemporary, he points out that each has been linked with Ephesus, thus suggesting that the same pastoral problem might have caused this theme to recur through these documents. 'The Gospel According to John vol II' (New York) 1970 p778.

15. Leslie Newbigin argues, 'This attempt to justify the fragmentations of Protestantism is not a legitimate exposition of the text. Jesus is praying for visible unity among those who believe. "If we walk in the light, as he is in the light, we have fellowship one with another" (1 John 1.7). The prayer of Jesus is for a unity which is a real participation of believers in the love and obedience which unites Jesus with the Father, a participation which is as invisible as the flow of sap which unites the branches with the vine, and which is at the same time as visible as the unity of branch and vine — as visible as the love and obedience of Jesus . . . this unity will enable the world to know the love of God not just as an idea or a doctrine but as a palpable reality experienced in the supernatural love which holds believers together in spite of all their human diversities.' 'The Light has Come: An exposition of the Fourth Gospel' (Grand Rapids) 1982, p235.

16. Schnackenburg also argues that the relationship is primarily one of mutual love, but he bases his interpretation on a linguistic link with 13.34. 'This linguistic similarity between the two texts points to a closeness of ideas, namely that the unity that is desired is brought about in reciprocal love'. R. Schnackenburg, 'The Gospel According to John vol III chapters 13-21' ET (London) 1982, p191.

THE ECUMENICAL DEBATE

Chapter Four

MULTIPLE HISTORY

When you lose your way there is little point in looking for your destination until you have discovered where you are. A map and compass will help, but you will first need to look for landmarks – not only the obvious ones in front of you, but the ones you passed getting to where you are. We must leave the question of what might serve us for map and compass until the next chapter. We first need to sort out where we are. For that we need to look back, not only for landmarks, but for a sense of the shape of our wanderings. In other words, we need to come to terms with our history if we are to understand the present reality of the church, let alone continue the search for God's tomorrow.

There will be those who say that they and their church are *not* lost. They know where they are, where they have been and some will even claim they know where they are going. We need to view such claims with a mixture of anxiety and compassion. Anxiety because such certainty is dangerous and compassion because people who can't acknowledge a need are not easy to help. There was surely sarcasm in his voice when Jesus said to the Pharisees, 'It is not the healthy who need a doctor, but the sick. I have not come to call the righteous, but sinners'. (Mark 2.17).

The call to repentance, to acknowledge what we are and to put our trust in God's transforming love, is not only a call to individual salvation, but an invitation for the whole people of God. To be satisfied with the state of the church (or even just my part of it) is to display the kind of triumphal pride that Paul saw in some of the Corinthian Christians: 'All of you, no doubt, have everything you could desire. You have come into your fortune already. You have come into your kingdom – and left us out.' (1 Corinthians 4.8 NEB).

There are two types of certainty which should worry us here. One says 'My church is right and the others are wrong', although it will often take a more liberal and subtle form, expressed in the old joke, 'You worship God in *your* way and I'll worship him in *his*'. The other certainty accepts the way things are and sees the disunity of the church as inevitable, spilt milk that isn't worthy of tears. There are even those who display pleasure in the wide range of consumer choice for the prospective member.[1]

We will return to the business of consumerism later, but the diversity of the church is very much a part of the present discussion. What is the difference between diversity and division? To find an answer we must go backwards. To understand ourselves we have to look at our history.

Looking Back

This is easier said than done. History is not only about listing facts, but about selecting and interpreting them. The historian stands at a particular place, with an agenda, priorities, assumptions and hopes. All these will affect which facts are selected and how those facts are interpreted. It becomes even more subjective when we look at a popular view of history, yet we must tackle these pictures of the past if we are to make sense of the present. Let me offer an example which we can use to think through some of the issues.

One view of church history sees it as a line through time. There may be branches and twists, but on the whole it is possible to trace a line back from the present to the beginning. We could debate where that beginning might be, but for the sake of argument we shall say the ministry of Jesus, when he called disciples to follow him. [2] It could be drawn something like diagram 1.

This is, of course, a simplified and stylized diagram which, as a pictorial chronology listing events, does not explain those events. But its point is not to provide an historical analysis of what happened but rather to present a pattern which many people will recognise as the kind of over-view they have of church history. If this picture in any way relates to how people understand the story so far, then we need to examine it with some care. We are not just dealing with the theories expounded and sharpened by experts, but how people in general see the way things are. Not only will popular understandings of history affect the way we view the present situation, but our understanding of the present situation will have an effect on the way we view our history.

This picture may be helpful for providing the framework within which a listing of historical events may be made — for example *when* a split occurred and *who* was involved. But there are many assumptions lurking just below the surface and we need to see how these assumptions affect the over-all pattern.

First, the fact that a single line emerges from the beginning suggests a time when there was only one church. Whether we see that as the churches represented in the New Testament or the first congregation in Jerusalem, there is a widespread belief in a *golden age*. The implications of this assumption may lead to the view that the story has gone downhill ever since (thus separating us from the people who inhabit the pages of the New Testament) or that the picture of the 'Church of the New Testament' is a pattern which we must seek to re-discover or impose on what we do today. Whether the argument is about baptism, the ordination of women or the need for elders, the belief in a golden age hovers in the background. But *was* there a golden age? Should we try to re-live what we find in the New Testament? There is a strong case to be made from within the New Testament itself that there never was a golden age, nor was there a single reality that we could call 'The Church of the New Testament'. How does such a claim affect what we make of our present circumstances?

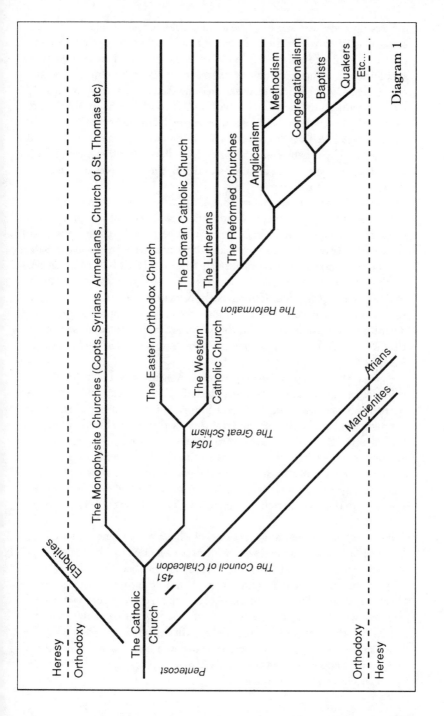

Diagram 1

Secondly, the picture suggests a single line of development. There *are* branches, some of which pass over the boundary into heresy, but these branches move in a line from one position to another. This must lead to terrible over-simplification, reducing complex movements in history to simple cause and effect. That in turn supports an *us and them* mentality, a view of church history which is reduced to 'goodies' and 'baddies'. Of course, many would want to see today's church in those terms, but if we are to face seriously the question of unity we need to listen to each other. Only then will we begin to understand the reasons why others are as they are and believe what they believe. This reminds us that encounter, discussion and dialogue are important aspects of the ecumenical movement.

Thirdly, there is the assumption that, if the diagram were seen to represent a tree, then the main trunk grows from the New Testament and proceeds to the person looking back. Perhaps a tree isn't a very good analogy because all trees end in branches! Perhaps we could think of a river. The people looking back believe that they are a part of the main stream and that the other traditions are the tributaries. Of course, this is easier to claim if you are part of a majority tradition like the Orthodox Church or the Roman Catholic Church, but you can still make such a claim even if you are the majority Church in a town or a country – or just because you think you are more right than somebody else! We all make the claim to some extent because we see history from where we are.

Again we have the problem of continuity. A picture made up of lines is not able to represent the variety of ways in which the Faith, and particular emphases of the Faith, are passed on. Protestant historians may want to trace a strand through the Catholic Church until it emerges with a split rather like a branch. On the other hand, they may wish to represent a strand prior to the visible emergence of their Protestant churches as a line which is preset at the beginning but goes 'underground' in the interim and is represented as a dotted line. An example may be the way in which a Baptist might see 'believer's baptism' as the norm in the early church only to be long ignored and then re-discovered at the Reformation.[3]

Fourthly, many would want to re-draw the lines representing the boundary between orthodoxy and heresy. Churches have tended to see themselves at the centre of orthodoxy (that's what *commitment* has been seen to be about) with the boundary then drawn in such a way as to include those nearest to them, but excluding others. The radius of acceptable divergence drawn around a church will vary according to how liberal it is. So some parts of the church would exclude others and the judgement might well be reciprocated. What the line picture doesn't do is demonstrate how each denomination includes a spectrum of opinion and practice which often overlaps in some ways with similar spectrums in other denominations.[4]

Finally, the diagram draws the boundary line as though there *is* a clear line and we know where to draw it. But heresy isn't that simple, and the more we accept diversity within the church the more acute becomes the question of identity. Do we define Christianity by drawing a circle around it, do we picture the history of the church as flowing within parallel lines, or do we search for some other means of determining what makes the church Christian?

If we return to the diagram, we could ask some questions about what is thought to be going on at the parting of the ways. What do the splits mean? Is the smaller group which leaves the larger group moving towards truth or towards heresy? How important are social, political and personality influences in what is going on? Should we see the split as the result of a renewal movement that doesn't find enough flexibility within the parent body and is forced to leave or decides it has no other option.[5] When a schism occurs should we plot the path on the diagram as one branch leaving the trunk, or in the form of a 'V'? Has one party *left* or have *both* moved apart?[6]

Now and Then

This extended study of church history has raised a great many questions. The exploration hasn't really been about history, as any self-respecting historian will no doubt quickly point out, but about how people see things. An over-simplified view of the past often walks hand in hand with an over-simplified view of the present. I have used the phrase *over-simplified* as a euphemism, because I could just as well say *bigoted*.

As there seem to be so many short-comings with this diagram, perhaps we should make another attempt. In diagram 2 (see p54), each circle represents a tradition within the world church: Orthodox, Catholic, Reformed and Pentecostal.

First, this picture shows us that there are areas of agreement shared by all. The church *is* recognizable in its very different forms and there is the hint of a common confession of faith which we shall have to explore further. The diagram also reminds us that this common ground is surrounded by areas of *bi-lateral* common ground where two traditions share an emphasis as well as having their own distinctive areas of difference.

Secondly, the diagram attempts to represent the relationship between different traditions. It is modestly successful in showing us the relative areas of overlap and distinctiveness, but it is not able to show us how much *variety* there is within each tradition. Because each circle is a flat, monochrome symbol, we are only shown that there is an area of overlap between various traditions. We are not shown that due to variety *within* each tradition, there will be some parts of one tradition and other parts of another tradition which have a closer degree of consensus with each other than with the other parts of their respective traditions.

For example, it is not just that Catholics in general have common ground

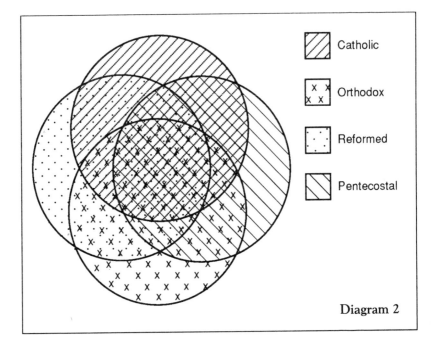

(hatched)	Catholic
(x marks)	Orthodox
(dotted)	Reformed
(diagonal)	Pentecostal

Diagram 2

with Anglicans in general, and Anglicans in general have common ground with Reformed churches in general. But those Anglicans who believe themselves and their church to be within the Catholic tradition, may well be *different* Anglicans from those who believe themselves and their church to be part of the Reformed tradition. On the other hand, there will be many Anglicans who will claim that they are in both traditions or, more strictly, that Anglicanism is Catholic *and* Reformed. This example could be repeated in each of the traditions for our diagram cannot deal with such complex, human realities!

Thirdly, the diagram suggests that each tradition has areas not shared by the others, as though there was no link between them. This would be a pessimistic view if it were to be overstated. What we need to see is that these distinctive areas are not *new* areas of belief quite different from what other Christians believe. Rather, each distinctive area can be seen as *a distinctive view of the Faith as a whole* and a distinctive perspective on the *centre* of the Faith which is shared with others. Thus each original aspect of a tradition can be interpreted as a view of the common Faith and, as a result, it can even be linked to the distinctive aspects of the other traditions. The centre is more than common ground, it actually *links* those unique areas of each tradition with each other.

For example, we could contrast the Catholic concern for celebrating the eucharist on a weekly or daily basis with the Presbyterian practice of far fewer opportunities for communion, even once a quarter or twice a year. Yet these different approaches to the sacrament share the common perspective of doing what they do because they believe the eucharist to be important. One tradition says that, because the eucharist is important, it must be shared *frequently*, while the other tradition says that because it is important, communion must be preserved as a significant, *special* event, prepared for, anticipated and remembered.

We must not gloss over the differences between these two views in terms of what they mean by the eucharist being *special*[7], but neither will we gain anything by ignoring the points of agreement. By saying that the eucharist is important, both are centring the Faith they confess, and the life they seek to live, in the life, death and resurrection of Jesus Christ. Ecumenical encounters often include such surprises, when Christians from different parts of the church discover, when hearing others account for their faith, that outward differences are often alternative cultural expressions of a shared concern.

Fourthly, just as the diagram doesn't show the diversity within each tradition, so it doesn't distinguish between different aspects of each tradition. The diagram is a blunt instrument which takes no account of theology over against worship, or mission over against spirituality. The diagram just states that there *are* areas of agreement and disagreement, but does not tell us what these might be.

Finally, the diagram only offers a *cross-section* through time, a frozen moment in the history of the church, whether that of today or the century before last. We are not offered a *story* which tells how we got to this point, but rather a picture of where we are now. This demonstrates the limitation of *any* diagram. Like a metaphor, it will have a main point of contact which illuminates reality but will not make contact at other points. Thus diagram 1 highlights a history of development, built upon division, but tells us little of the present relationships between the churches. Diagram 2 tells us something of these present relationships, but nothing of their history.

Yet even within the main point of each diagram there is a lack of subtlety, based both upon the simplicity of a two-dimensional drawing and the over-simplified assumptions on the part of those observations which are being expressed visually. Indeed, this last point is their main usefulness. The diagrams do not so much represent *reality* as particular *views* of reality and therefore highlight the assumptions, often false or inadequate, which seem to undergird such views. Here we have a historical *via negativa* which at least exorcises some unpleasant spectres, even if it doesn't provide us with an adequate historical picture.

The questions continue to present themselves. How do we identify orthodoxy, or to put it another way, how do we describe what it means to be a Christian or to be a valid expression of the Christian Church? Do we identify the answer with our own position, with our church as the sun and those planets that are close enough included in our solar system? Do we set limits and if so *how* do we set them? Do we accept a consensus as making up the Christian Church and if so how do we agree that consensus? Do we construct a creed or confession of faith and welcome any who are able to assent to its test? Do we concern ourselves more with behaviour than with theology and point out to all the church that the real issue is discipleship and faithfulness to Christ, rather than a set of abstract principles. [8]

In 1987 Basil Hume, the Cardinal Archbishop of Westminster and leader of the Roman Catholic Church in England and Wales, made a statement about his Church's commitment to the search for unity. In what was immediately hailed as a historic speech he spoke about the nature of the unity we should seek and used the phrase 'legitimate diversity'. [9] We could sum up many of the questions that have been thrown up so far by asking 'What do we mean by the word *legitimate* when we use the phrase *legitimate diversity*?

The first assumption of diagram 1 was of a golden age at the beginning of the history of the church. Most churches seem to identify with such a time and seek to find their own practices and beliefs reflected in such an age. In other words, the early church is claimed by each tradition as its own. So a view of the golden age is linked with the churches' self-understanding. An examination of this assumption will not only be an excursion into history but a challenge to assumptions we make about today.

Golden Age or Fellow Pilgrims?

There is a temptation to read the Bible in a flat way which gives each story and each statement the same weight and which irons out all the differences. Somehow we feel that, as the Word of God, the Bible must have a unity whereby everything hangs together and each piece dovetails into the next. Yet the same Spirit who inspired the biblical authors to bear witness to their faith and their understanding of the story of Jesus also worked in the wider church community in its recognition of certain books as the canon of Scripture. Through the writing, through the recognition of the canon and through the Spirit working in believer and church today, there is an *event* which we may call 'the Word of God'. This word is not dead on a page, but alive as we receive it and act upon it in our own situation. We will miss a great deal if we read the Bible as though it were all uttered in the same tone of voice and we will ignore the special gifts of its writers if we assume that they are all saying the same thing. When, at the end of the second century, the church came to recognize four Gospels as being of special importance, it was significant that there were *four* not *one*. [10]

While we might think of the different books as parts of the one New Testament, we must remind ourselves that they were written by different authors, for different readers and at different times. There may be a time-span of sixty or seventy years [11] in the writing of the various books, but even more important than this are the different situations in which they came to be written. The books were written in different parts of the Mediterranean world in order to respond to particular, and therefore various, pastoral needs. When we add to this the variety of cultures and religious philosophies that went to make up what has been called 'the melting pot of the Mediterranean' we may begin to see new patterns in what are familiar verses.

It is possible to benefit by reading the letters of Paul 'cold' – listening to the words as they strike us, with no further explanation. But an awareness of what the problems and needs were in the various churches will enable us to understand and receive so much more. They were written for different situations – so we need to understand their relevance for Corinth or Rome or Thessalonica if we are more fully to discover their relevance for us today.

While the four gospels tell the same story they do not tell it in the same way. Not only is there disagreement about the order of some of the events [12] but some stories are left out (or were not known) and some sayings appear in different contexts and with different interpretations. [13] The most obvious difference is in the way in which John's Gospel comprises long speeches while the other gospels are made up of smaller units pieced together. Tradition has long identified each gospel with a different place [14] and understood the different emphases of the gospels as relating to the needs of each of those places. But each book is different not only because of the audience but because of the relationship between the writer and the audience. In each case we have not so much a rebuttal of what was believed in a particular place as an affirmation of the Gospel which uses positively the emphases of a particular church. For example, it is likely that Matthew wrote his Gospel for a church made up of conservative Jewish Christians. He portrays Jesus as the one who doesn't break but fulfils the Law, a new Moses [15] who, through the cross and resurrection, leads his people from slavery and in his teaching offers them a new way of life.

While this rich variety of different emphases is placed together between the covers of one Bible, we must remember that when they were written, and for many decades afterwards, this was not the case. At first, each congregation might well have had only one book, be it a letter of Paul or a gospel. We might try to blend the books, but the people for whom they were written were not able to do so. We therefore need to see each book as a presentation of the Christian Gospel, written for particular people and in a particular way. When we do this, we see them in a new light and also begin to see the differences between them. Not only do they show different theological emphases, but they point us to churches with different attitudes on church life and mission. There was variety from the beginning as Christians differed over their attitude to the cultures and philosophies around them.

It isn't easy to piece together a clear picture of the early years. We may disagree about whether to emphasize the unity or the diversity which is reflected in the New Testament. But because our task is to face up to the issue of *unity*, we need first to come to terms with the *diversity* of the New Testament material.

The *Biblical Theology* approach of former years attempted to integrate the biblical material in such a way as to provide the biblical teaching on different subjects. More recent New Testament studies have tended to highlight the distinctive theological emphases of the different writers. There is now a concern to avoid harmonizing voices which should be heard making distinct contributions in differing contexts. To talk of different *schools* in the New Testament would be to suggest far too static a concept. We should rather think of lines of development which are to be seen sometimes evolving separately, sometimes in dialogue and sometimes in tension.

For example, C.K. Barrett has suggested three different post-Pauline strains to be detected through an analysis of those New Testament books related to Paul. These are the Pastoral Epistles and Ephesians, both with a heavy, though distinctively different, dependence on the written works of Paul, and Luke/Acts, which presents him as the apostle to the Gentiles, though never suggesting that he was the author of numerous epistles.[16] These works suggest different audiences as well as different solutions to common problems. Similarly, we see Hebrews, 1 Peter, James and Matthew each addressing the issue of the church's relationship to Judaism in a different way.

The picture which emerges from a contrasting of the theologies of the different New Testament books is of a period of creative and fermenting development. The word which is now used to indicate these differing developments is *trajectory* which offers the picture of a series of flight paths, related to each other in complex ways. In this connection, R.H. Fuller suggests that orthodoxy may be viewed 'not as static but as directional'[17] and this may help us as we struggle with a variety of 'trajectories' today. For example, it has long been recognised that there were tensions between the Palestinian and Hellenistic strands of early Christianity. It has been suggested that this tension was not only to be found between the Jerusalem church and Antioch and the Gentile mission, but that in Jerusalem itself there were two distinct Christian communities.[18]

J.D.G. Dunn, in his comprehensive study 'Unity and Diversity in the New Testament', suggests that the New Testament provides a number of streams of Christian experience and theology. He sees *Early Catholicism* as one stream amongst several and offers reasons why this particular trajectory gained an ascendant in the second century, in preference, for example, to *Apocalyptic Christianity*. Although the *Catholic* stream is the one which becomes the mainstream in later centuries, he argues that our understanding of Christian identity today must take account of the variety of streams present in the early years.

If taken to an extreme position, each stream may become heretical. Dunn points out that heresies of the second century, such as the extreme Judaisers known as Ebionites [19], were an extension of the stream we know as Jewish or Palestinian Christianity. Similarly, Gnosticism [20] may be seen as the end of a stream which is present in the New Testament, rather than a hard position to be seen in opposition to the biblical writers. We can see how, for example, the Fourth Gospel uses in a positive way the very Hellenistic culture which has led some of its likely readers astray. It is as if the writer is portraying Jesus in the thought forms of the would-be Gnostic while ensuring that the Hellenization stays within certain limits. As a result, Jesus is portrayed as the revelation of God's glory, the divine Son of God, but any tendency towards a *docetic* christology, which would deny his true humanity, is resisted. The divine Word does not masquerade as flesh, but becomes flesh. The death of Jesus is central to the Gospel and that death is graphically portrayed with the gory description of blood and water flowing from a pierced side. Here is a daring presentation of the gospel which does not turn its back on contemporary culture but engages it and affirms it while also affirming the distinctiveness of the Christian message.

Whereas the previous generation of biblical scholars would attempt to construct a fairly uniform picture of New Testament teaching around such themes as the person of Christ, ministry, patterns of worship and the sacraments, Dunn is now representative of the contemporary concern to highlight the distinctiveness of the various traditions. Yet there is also a desire to grapple with the nature of *unity* in the New Testament. The relationship of various of confessions of faith in the New Testament will serve as a convenient illustration which we will also be able to use later in our discussion.

This desire to identify distinctive theological trends helps us to recognize different ways of expressing the importance of Jesus:

> 'In simplified terms . . . we may say that "Jesus is the Messiah" appears to have been the chief confession of Palestinian Jewish Christians, "Jesus is the Son of God" of Hellenistic Jewish Christians, "Jesus is Lord" of Gentile Christians.' [21]

This picture is qualified by suggesting that each confession was the most important in each context rather than the only one. Each was probably important because it was 'the most meaningful and relevant expression of the Christian faith in that context'. It is inevitable that different words, important in different cultural situations, would not only provide the language content of the various confessions but also contribute something to their respective meanings.

You will notice that in each of the confessions cited above there is a common theme and herein lies the unity which is to be found in the wide diversity of the New Testament witnesses. The common theme is, of course, *Jesus*. There are two points to be made here. First, all the confessions are in the present tense for Jesus is the living reality who is the focus of the life of the church. Secondly, *Jesus* is not an abstract principle or mythical cypher, but the Jesus of Nazareth who was crucified and whom God raised.

Amidst the diversity which we have been able to highlight only briefly, the consistent strand is the affirmation that the man Jesus is to be identified with the risen Lord. This may seem a rather tame conclusion but it is fundamental not only in linking the various presentations of the Gospel with each other but in linking them with the pre-Easter proclamation of Jesus himself. This is the centre from which the various expressions of Christianity radiate. We shall return to ask whether this affirmation provides the basis for a definitive creed, but here we need to note something even more basic than that. We need to see that in the New Testament the promise and experience of salvation which are expressed in different ways in different situations, and the awareness of the divine reality transforming lives, are always earthed in the historical reality of Jesus of Nazareth. Here is no disembodied philosophy or vague religious emotion. All is centred on the Jesus whom we crucified but whom God raised from the dead.

Diversity or Division?

The New Testament confronts us with the issue of unity in another way, for as well as providing a central affirmation about Jesus Christ, the Bible also challenges us to face up to the very fact of the canon itself. An important aspect of the unity of the New Testament is the unity of being Scripture, recognized by the church as the Word of God. The Spirit who bore witness to God's saving action in Jesus, by inspiring the diverse witnesses of the New Testament, is the same Spirit who has inspired the church to recognize these writings as Scripture. Whether we wish to accept the thesis of strong areas of distinctiveness within the pages of the New Testament, or whether we wish to argue for a closer harmony, the fact that they all are Scripture is important. The word *harmony* is an interesting one for unlike *unison*, you can only have harmony when people are singing different notes. The fact that different expressions of the Faith and different ways of being the church are together in the canon of Scripture is of very great importance. The canon of Scripture recognizes the validity of diversity and therefore the validity of very different expressions of Christianity.

By embracing a variety of forms of expression of the Christian faith, the canon of Scripture makes possible a multiplicity of confessions within the church. However, once we recognize this, we must move on to acknowledge its corollary. If the diversity of the New Testament makes possible a diversity of forms of Christian expression, then in doing so it also *relativizes* those expressions. Once we have acknowledged this diversity, we can no longer make absolute claims for one particular expression of the Christian Faith. While we will inevitably justify our own church's position by an appeal to Scripture, we must now recognize that such an appeal cannot be absolute or exclusive. Having found diversity in Scripture we must face the validity of other expressions of being the church than our own. [22]

How then are we to respond to the testimony of Scripture? In particular, what are the implications for church doctrine and order? For example, the 'is/ought' dilemma is never far below the surface. [23] There are theological statements about the church in the New Testament and there are descriptions of what the church did. What status do these have for us? In what sense are they authoritative for present church life? Should we try to duplicate what is described in the book of Acts? These questions of method are vital, for example, in our contemporary debates about the ordination of women, interpretations of the sacraments and the ecumenical enterprise as a whole.

The very diversity of the New Testament leads us to two important decisions. First, we should not try to find or create *one* rigid form of church life or expression of the Gospel. Even when Paul is arguing strongly against what he believes to be wrong tendencies in the various churches, he does not unchurch his opponents, nor does he claim that they are no longer Christians. It is an argument within the family and often he will use the language and thought forms of his opponents in an attempt to deal positively with their concerns. [24]

Secondly, the recognition of diversity must neither be misunderstood nor misused. For some it would be tempting to accept the argument that the great variety within the New Testament is a justification of the present disunity of the church. While the multiplicity of confessions relativizes the claim of any one church, it should also lead that church from the implicit claims of its own exclusive rightness into the ecumenical forum. It is not enough for a church vaguely to accept others while remaining unchanged itself.

The canon of Scripture *recognizes* the diversity which it sees as part of the providence of God and the rich cultural and imaginative variety of humanity. However, the present disunity of the church is built upon the assumption of *non-recognition*. It is one thing to acknowledge the existence of other Christians, it is quite another to recognize their doctrine, worship and church life as equally valid as your own. Such a recognition is a radical departure from where we are even now. Agreed statements between churches are very important, but we must always acknowledge the tension between the ecumenical vision of such verbal formulae and the non-verbal claims implicit in the exclusive structures of the churches which have seemed to reach agreement. Our churches have grown and developed in particular historical and cultural circumstances. They have institutions and patterns whose purpose is to enable the status quo to continue. So what does it mean to recognize other churches while keeping the same structures which maintain the status quo?

There are two things which follow from this. One is the need for reconciliation between churches and the other is a theology of the church which is able to cope with such plurality. These two needs belong together. In order for two church traditions to accept each other they need a wider framework which justifies and gives purpose to such a task. Equally, a wider view of the diversity of the church needs to be earthed in the experience of particular attempts at reconciliation.

We would do well to return to the New Testament, for there we can find examples of how, in particular situations, *limits* were set on the range of diversity. Those writers who addressed positively the various streams running through the New Testament churches also set limits on what was possible. For example, Matthew, writing for conservative Jewish Christians and Paul, writing to young churches grappling with Gnosticism, set limits to the direction in which the audience was moving. There were two tests to be put – *if worship of God was no longer determined by Jesus of Nazareth and his resurrection, or if diversity led to a breach of love towards others who also called on the name of Jesus, then diversity was judged to have gone too far.* 'The centre also determined the circumference'.[25] The heart of the Faith which centred on Jesus and his way was also the boundary which determined the identity of the community of Jesus. In so far as many of the main streams of the Christian church have not displayed love to all those who call on the name of Jesus, it can be argued that they have stepped outside the boundaries of New Testament Christian identity. The New Testament is concerned both for *orthodoxy* (a faith centred in Jesus the Christ) and *orthopraxy* (the way that we treat each other).

Ecumenism can never just be a matter of theological dialogue and convergence – it must also take account of how we treat each other, both in our external actions and the implicit claims of our unreconciled church orders and patterns of life. But just as the two are linked in the New Testament – *faith in Jesus and living the love of Jesus* – so dialogue and agreement are linked with our treatment of each other. The theology gives a framework in which love can grow, and love gives direction and drive to the theological quest.[26]

But there is something else which we must learn from the diversity of the New Testament. The diversity is caused by *mission*, for it is the result of the Gospel entering different situations and engaging with different cultures. We will need to remember this when we discuss confessions of faith and mission itself. For now we need to make some observations along the way.

First, the diversity of the New Testament proclamation leads us to see that there is no such thing as a theoretical, disembodied gospel. The Gospel is good news and, because news is *relevant information*, the Gospel must always be expressed in ways that are *relevant* to a particular situation. This question of relevance does not mean that a theoretical gospel exists, hovering in mid-air and waiting to be applied to the 'real world'. The very words that are used to express the Gospel bring meaning with them, and so the whole process is one of *incarnation*. The Word has become flesh, Jewish flesh, first century flesh, particular flesh. The Word continues to become flesh, but the form of its incarnation will change with the raw materials of the Body of Christ in a particular culture.

Secondly, something which is relevant to one situation may well not be relevant to another. A hymn tune written in the musical style of the 1950's is very dated by the time you reach the 1990's. The more relevant an expression of the Faith is for one culture, the more it will need to be adapted for another. In the nineteenth century it was *European* Christianity which seemed to be exported around the world. But the proclamation of the Gospel within other cultures was often overlooked, and, as a result, people in the churches of Latin America, Africa and Asia are still struggling with the business of an authentic proclamation in their own culture.

The acceptance of diversity in the New Testament means a recognition of this embeddedness of the Gospel in each situation. This in turn means that there is a need for *development*. When we see the way in which the Gospel is expressed for one particular situation we also take on board an acceptance that expressions of the Gospel will need to develop when they are explored in new situations. [27]

Thirdly, if we return to our chronological chart of church history in diagram 1, we are able to see that sometimes a split occurred because of the need to adapt to a new situation (and the reluctance of some parts of the church to accept such change). There is enough truth in this for us to recognize that the battles of the past were fought on battle grounds that may well no longer be around. The abuses of one generation which led to a prophetic protest and then a break may well no longer exist. We need to clarify the reasons for our present diversity, not least because we may discover that we are each still expressing the Gospel in a way which was relevant for a past situation but not for today. There is a poem by the Welsh poet R.S. Thomas which describes an aspect of his nation's life which disturbs him greatly:

> '. . . an impotent people,
> Sick with inbreeding,
> Worrying the carcass of an old song'. [28]

Leaving Wales aside, it is a description that is too close for comfort in many of our church situations.

Finally, we are reminded that the context of New Testament diversity is *mission*. If the church had stayed in Jerusalem amongst one type of person it might have avoided all sorts of problems, though it is unlikely. The ultimate rejection of the Ebionites was a rejection of a form of Jewish Christianity which had failed to develop. When we recognize this, we are led to see that even conservatism can be heretical and that *faithfulness needs to look forward as well as back*. Mission will always involve risk and will need to be based on genuine faith. It will mean taking seriously the people and culture in which the proclamation is to happen. Mission must always be the context in which ecumenism works, whether we are talking about the united witness of churches in a common situation or the prophetic witness of love and hope to which the whole church is called in a despairing and endangered world.

We may not have finally decided where we are on our journey, but we have begun to identify the lie of the land. We have begun to recognize the variety of the landscape and we now need to seek the map and compass which will help us forward. So we must look at the same territory again but this time from a different perspective.

Now we must face the question of creeds and confessions. If we take seriously the incarnate nature of all theology and church life then what are we to make of the creeds of the church? How are we to express our faith today? Must we be resigned to a vague sentiment of wishful thinking and tolerance or are we able to confess the faith boldly? And if we see the New Testament Church wrestling with the way it proclaims the Gospel, are there marks of such a struggle going on in our own generation?

Notes

1. This acceptance of the situation as it is can also be born of despair. First, it can arise out of the belief that things cannot change and sinful division is inevitable. It can arise out of a distrust of hope. Yet Christian hope should always be linked to the call of God. If he is calling us to seek the peace of his Kingdom then who are we to wash our hands of the task, or argue that it is impossible?

2. It could be argued that the church began at Pentecost. But our interest is historical and the people who received the Spirit and proclaimed the resurrection in Acts 2 were the ones who had already responded to the call of Jesus in his lifetime and witnessed his cross and exaltation.

3. Some attempts have been made to trace a 'dotted line' of witness in the centuries between the early church and the Reformation. See J.M. Cramp, 'Baptist History: from the foundation of the Christian Church to the present day' (London) 1871 and J.T. Christian, 'A History of the Baptists' (Nashville) 1922.

4. In fact the question of Christian identity which is raised by the diversity of churches is also a question debated *within* denominations eg. Stephen Sykes, 'The Integrity of Anglicanism' (London) 1978 and Brian Haymes,

'A Question of Identity: Reflections on Baptist Principles and Practice' (Yorkshire Baptist Association) 1986.

5. Methodists existed within and alongside the Church of England for a long time and it was only after the death of John Wesley that the final break came.

6. An interpretation of the split is bound to be tied up with a view of what 'orthodoxy' means. If it is seen as faithfulness to a tradition then the split will be viewed in a different way from someone who sees orthodoxy as faithfulness to the testimony of Scripture interpreted 'under the Holy Spirit'.

7. The way in which each tradition will regard the eucharist as *special* will reflect its interpretation of what is *happening* in the sacrament. Here we may notice distinctive understandings of the operation of grace: different emphases on the use of material or sacramental means on the one hand or the use of words leading to and supporting faith of the heart on the other. Yet even here we may observe that there will be Catholic concern to emphasize the historical remembrance and the place of personal faith in the eucharist, just as there will be Presbyterians wanting to find in the use of bread and wine an affirmation about the presence of the risen Christ and the on-going place of incarnation in the purposes of God.

8. In recent years, and especially amongst Third World theologians, much has been made of the words *orthodoxy* and *orthopraxy*. (Greek *orthos* = right; *doxa* = judgement, opinon, estimation; *praxus* = deed, act. Therefore *orthodoxy* = 'right thinking' and *orthopraxy* or *orthopraxis* = 'right action'). See also Hans Kung, 'The Church Maintained in Truth: A Theological Meditation' ET (London) 1980 eg. p36: 'The totality of faith consists in the integrity of commitment, not in completely correct propositions'.

9. The statement was made in the course of a debate at the British Conference held at the Swanwick Conference Centre from 31 August to 4 September 1987. It was the culmination of the first three years of the Inter-Church Process 'Not Strangers but Pilgrims'.

10. It seems that in the second century churches used to read from the Jewish Scriptures plus any Christian writing they had. These latter writings would differ from place to place but between 170 and 200AD there were attempts in various places to agree a list of books. Some queried the Johannine writings while others included such works as 'The Gospel of Peter'. The *Muratorian Canon*, in particular, dates from the end of the second century and may well have been an episcopal document originating in Rome. It seems to be a list intended as guidance for the wider church. But into the fourth century there were still disagreements about the inclusion of certain books (eg. Revelation in the East and Hebrews in the West). See J.G. Davies, 'The Early Church' (London) 1965 pp85f and W.H.C Frend, 'The Rise of Christianity' (London) 1984 pp250f.

11. From about 50AD (I Thessalonians) to the early decades of the second century. Scholars, of course, disagree about the dating of particular books and especially the time when the later ones were written.

12. For example the Cleansing of the Temple comes at the beginning of Holy Week in the Synoptic Gospels (Matthew, Mark and Luke) whereas it appears at the beginning of the ministry in John (2.13ff). In John, the dating of the crucifixion is different from the Synoptics.

13. For example there is no account of the Last Supper in John's Gospel, yet for the same evening in the upper room he describes the story of the foot-washing (John 13.1-17) which appears nowhere else. The saying about this generation having no sign other than the sign of Jonah refers to the witness of preaching in Luke 16.30-32, whereas Matthew 12.39-41 sees a parallel between the three days in the belly of the fish and the sign of the resurrection. Matthew 16.4 is less clear.

14. For example John has been linked with Ephesus and Mark with Rome. Matthew has been both linked with Caesarea and Syrian Antioch, but usually a congregation of Jewish Christians trying to come to terms with their relationship to Judaism and the Law. Though Luke has a less firm tradition, some link him with Greece, but this reflects more the traditions about the evangelist than anything else. While these theories may on occasion be fanciful and far from proveable, their importance is that they reflect an awareness that each Gospel was written in a different context in response to different needs.

15. The teaching of Jesus in Matthew is placed in five main blocks which many have linked with the five books of Moses, the Pentateuch. The first collection of sayings is the Sermon on the Mount which could be seen as echoing Moses receiving the Commandments on Mount Sinai. In Jesus we have a new Moses and a new law which is the fulfilment of the old.

16. C.K. Barrett, 'Acts and the Pauline Corpus', 'Expository Times' 88 (1966-67) pp2-5.

17. R.H. Fuller, 'New Testament Trajectories and Biblical Authority', 'Studia Evangelica' VII (Berlin: Akademie) 1982 cited in R.E. Brown, 'The Church the Apostles Left Behind', (London) 1984 p18n.

18. See James D. Dunn, 'Unity and Diversity in the New Testament: An inquiry into the character of earliest Christianity' (London) 1977. He suggests that Hellenistic Jews (those who spoke Greek, rather than Aramaic or Hebrew, as their daily language) maintained separate synagogues in Jerusalem. Thus the first Christians came from two distinct Jewish groups – the Hebrews and the Hellenists. *The seven* in Acts 6.5 were probably all Hellenists and might well have been the existing leaders of the Hellenistic Jewish Christian community. For Dunn's case concerning tension between the two groups see pp268-275.

19. The Ebionites were a Jewish Christian sect who were separate from the church by the second century and denounced. They had a 'reduced' doctrine of the Person of Christ, believing that his special status came from the descent of the Spirit at his baptism. They followed an extremely rigorous view of the Mosaic Law and only accepted the Gospel of Matthew.

20. Gnosticism was a complex religious movement which we know most about through the second century writings of those who opposed it. While Christian Gnosticism seems to have grown out of the church, it had become separate from the church by the end of the second century. The beliefs were a combination of various religious ideas from Greek, Persian and Christian sources, but the central idea was that of *gnosis* or knowledge. This secret knowledge was supposed to be revealed by God and made known to the initiates, (those 'in the know'), thus securing their eternal destiny. There was also a strong division between the spiritual and material worlds which led to a docetic christology.

21. Dunn 'Unity and Diversity' p58.

22. In 1951 the Lutheran scholar Ernst Kasemann argued that the New Testament 'provides the basis for the multiplicity of the confesssions': 'The canon of the New Testament and the Unity of the Church' reprinted in E. Kasemann, 'Essays on New Testament Themes' ET (London) 1964 pp95-107. See also his presentation to the World Conference for Faith and Order in Montreal in 1963 reprinted in E. Kasemann, 'New Testament Questions of Today' ET (London) 1969 pp252-259. Compare R.E. Brown's presentation to the same conference 'The Unity and Diversity in New Testament Ecclesiology' reprinted in R.E. Brown, 'New Testament Essays' (London) 1965 and the discussion of Kasemann's position in G. Ebeling, 'The Word of God and Tradition' ET (London) 1968 pp148-159. See also S. Sykes, 'The Identity of Christianity' (London) 1984 especially chapter one: 'Identity and Conflict in Christianity'.

23. *Is/ought* is a way of talking about hidden and incorrect assumptions. That something *is* the case does not mean that it *ought* to be the case. A description of what happened in a Bible story does not mean that we *ought* to copy those actions today. It may be that we ought to, but there need to be reasons given for doing so.

24. For example, his contrasting of law and gospel, talk of a 'spiritual' body in 1 Corinthians 15 and his talking about Jesus coming in the 'likeness' of flesh (Rom. 8.3; Phil. 2.7) were all texts which the second century Gnostics used to claim that they were following Paul. He is not a Gnostic and often criticises them, but the affinity which later Gnostics felt for his writing suggests that he was engaged in a positive dialogue with the Gnostics of his day.

25. Dunn, 'Unity and Diversity' p379. For his summary and subsequent discussion of diversity and the canon see pp370-388.

26. See H. Meyer and L. Vischer (ed.), 'Growth in Agreement (Geneva) 1984 which provides all the official bilateral reports between 1971 and 1982; also 'God's Reign – Our Unity' (London) 1984, the Anglican-Reformed report. See also the text of the multilateral Faith and Order 'Lima text', 'Baptism, Eucharist and Ministry' (Geneva) 1982.

27. Dunn argues (p381) that the canon recognizes the *process* of development. The *how* is shown us in the interaction between the church's faith in Jesus and its perceptions of the various challenges of contemporary life. It does not give us the *what* of development. 'The New Testament as canon demonstrates how the unifying centre of Christian faith came to diverse expression in the diverse circumstances of the first century; it does not dictate what the expression of Christian faith should be in any and every circumstance.'

28. 'Welsh Landscape' by R.S. Thomas in 'Collected Poems 1948-1968 (London) 1973 p9.

Chapter Five

CONFESSING ONE LORD

Visiting a shack in a Brazillian favella, where a group of people had gathered to study the Bible and explore its implications in the struggle for justice, many of us would recognize that here was the *church*. If we travelled to Mount Athos and entered the stillness and prayer of one of its Orthodox monasteries, we would experience something very different, but we would still use the word *church*. Similarly, in Britain, we would use the word *church* to describe both the gothic glory of a sung cathedral Evensong and the exuberance of a charismatic house group. These are all very different examples of the life of the church, but most of us would still see them as outcrops of the same spiritual reality – the people of God.

In our brief survey of the New Testament we saw how the very canon of Scripture contains and recognizes a diversity of expression of the Christian gospel. While we began to see a unifying feature in statements about and commitment to Jesus, we need to work some more at this business of diversity and unity.

Diversity or Division?
What is the difference between *diversity* and *division*? Are they just two words which different people might use to describe the same reality? The argument has long been advanced that the diversity within the church is a natural expression of the diversity of human culture and temperament. This is a valid and important point. But if the argument continues from here to see *all* the distinctions within the church in this way, then we will be guilty of crying 'Peace, peace' when there is no peace.

A quick glance at the history of the church is unlikely to produce a picture of groups agreeing to differ but remaining in fellowship with each other. Instead, what we will see is the fragmentation of the people of God – alienation, anathemas and schism. The words *diversity* and *division* do not just refer to the objective interpretation of a neutral observer, but to the way the various parts of the church view their relationships with each other. There is little point in using the word *diversity* to describe the difference between two churches who have each previously regarded the other as heretical and who still view each other with suspicion. That is *division* and it needs to be healed.

In the language of traditional theological reflection we could observe that we are here talking about the differences between the doctrines of Creation and the Fall. There is much variety which we can attribute to the glorious provision of God's gift in creation. But there is also a variety that is the result of human *sin*. It is caused by pride, fear or any number of the human sins which push people apart. The sin of division may be found within a local congregation, or it may be found between international church bodies. All Christians belong to *denominations*, parts of the church which are in some sense cut off from other parts of the church. We usually look back positively on the beginnings of our own tradition: we interpret its distinctive structures and activities as the necessary channel through which witness could be made to the truths, or that view of the truth, which we hold dear. But at some point a line is crossed between diversity and division. Historically, it may have come at the point of schism or break, but it is more likely to be a line that is frequently crossed. The continuing existence of denominations sets up a situation which is more likely to create relationships of division rather than relationships of openness and sharing. What we need are structures of fellowship rather than structures of division — but we must return to this later.

We have recognized variety within the New Testament, but it is important to remind ourselves about the causes of that variety. We saw that the diverse expressions of the Christian Faith were caused by the *missionary* need to express the Christian gospel in different cultural situations. The diversity was caused by the need to meet people and situations where they were. We can see this is a right extension of the ministry of Jesus who got alongside people, communicating with them in ways which they could understand, meeting them at the point of their need and sharing in the companionship of their tables. Paul developed this missionary identification as an expression of the gospel when he said:

> 'I am free and own no master; but I have made myself everyone's servant, to
> win over as many as possible. To Jews I behaved like a Jew, to win Jews; that
> is, to win those under the law I behaved as if under the law, though not myself
> subject to the law. To win those outside that law, I behaved as if outside, though
> not myself outside God's law, but subject to the law of Christ. To the weak
> I became weak, to win the weak. To them all I have become everything in turn,
> so that in one way or another I may save some. All this I do for the sake of the
> gospel, to have a share in its blessings'. (1 Corinthians 8.19-23)

We can soon see the difference between the diversity of the New Testament and the divisions of today if we look at a local situation. Paul wrote his letters to the church in a particular place: 'God's church at Corinth, dedicated to him in Christ Jesus, called to be his people' (Corinthians 1.2) or 'all of you in Rome who are loved by God and called to be his people' (Romans 1.7). He could speak of the '*churches* of Galatia' (Galatians 1.2) because Galatia was a region and would thus contain numerous towns, each with its own congregation. When, as at Corinth, tendencies within a congregation threatened to break it apart, Paul appealed to the Christians to see and use all their gifts and concerns within the perspective of God's love. So the diversity of the church in the New Testament is primarily a diversity of *place*.

However, if we look at a local town today we see many congregations, each representing on the local scene international bodies or traditions which differ from each other for historical, theological, political or social reasons. Methodist, Pentecostal, Anglican, Roman Catholic: we find a diversity of *type* rather than a diversity of *place*. In other words, we find a *division* according to type which is based upon a variety of factors quite different from the need to express the Gospel in the local culture.

In chapter 4 we saw the theory advanced that there were two church communities in Jerusalem from the earliest days of the church. Does not this assertion challenge the pattern in the New Testament of one church in each place which has just been presented? And if we can demonstrate two communities in tension in Jerusalem does not that have as much right to be normative for the church of today as one church in each place?

The two communities in Jerusalem are claimed to have arisen out of two quite distinct ethnic groups: those Jews who spoke Aramaic as their everyday language and those Jews who spoke Greek and worshipped in a separate synagogue. While we have one city, we have two quite distinct communities where language and culture need to express the Faith in different ways. Perhaps we could widen our claim for diversity in the New Testament by reminding ourselves that diversity was caused by the need to express the gospel in different *situations*, whether they were different geographical or different cultural places. In fact, it was the cultural differences which were even more likely to create the need for differing expressions of the gospel than the change of location. [1]

If the theory of tensions between the groups in Jerusalem is accepted, that still doesn't mean that we slavishly copy such behaviour today. Here is an important principle in how we use Scripture as a means of guiding our present day church life. The Bible often shows us examples of people who, though called by God, often failed to live up to their calling in every respect. Tension in Jerusalem is not a justification for tension today. When we examine the pattern of church life in the New Testament, what we find does not automatically become authoritative for us today. We need to test the story of the church against its own testimony as to the nature of its call.

In other words, the followers of Jesus Christ need to be continually compared with the Lord who gives identity to the community which bears his name. As we explore the other parts of the New Testament a fuller picture (or pictures) emerges which makes claims on our behaviour as the church for today. We have returned to creation and fall. The *creation* of the church, its life and possibilities, finds its meaning in Jesus Christ. Even the church of the New Testament must be tested against its Lord before we can follow in its way.

If we come back to our contemporary local town we may well point out that the number of Christians is too many for one congregation. Indeed there may well be different ethnic and cultural situations represented in the one town. This development also seems to have happened in the years after the writing of the New Testament. A number of congregations existed in a single place, but they were not separate churches. They had full fellowship together and this was expressed by their having one bishop who was the focus of their unity, especially in his role of teaching the faith and presiding at the eucharist.[2]

The situation today is very different. Denominational *structures* encourage fellowship between churches in one town with similar churches in another town, but often not with Christians in the same place.

We can see that denominations came into existence in particular times in the life of the church in response to particular situations. We can leave aside for the moment the issue as to whether the schism which brought them into institutional existence was the fault of the leavers or of those who were left. Suffice it to say, it could be argued that the denominations can in a positive sense be seen as distinct cultural expressions of the Christian faith. However, even if we can view them in this way, we need to recognize that circumstances have changed. The cultural or historical situation that caused a particular form of Christianity to emerge may no longer exist.

If you go to Thot in the Dordogne region of France you will find a wild life park that contains most of the breeds of animal which can be seen depicted in the local caves in paintings which may be fifteen thousand years old. The park is a living museum of animals that lived long ago, adapted to conditions that have long changed. Denominations often seem to be living museums testifying to conditions long changed and situations long altered. If the causes of division four hundred years ago no longer exist, then what are the implications for the way in which we live together as God's people? One of the problems is that when we begin to live apart, new reasons for our separateness arise. Distance creates suspicion, insularity breeds fear and both destroy love and trust.

In the fourth chapter of his letter to the Romans, Paul is arguing that both Gentile and Jewish Christians can see themselves as the descendants of Abraham. He shows how Abraham trusted God. His rabbinic argument then points out that Abraham's acceptance by God was before the time when God called him to institute circumcision as a mark of belonging to the people of God. Thus Abraham was accepted on the strength of his faith in God, the faith that had brought him in old age from the security of Harran to the insecurity of wandering in a strange land. Paul goes on to argue that those who are truly the children of Abraham are not those who are physically descended from him or who have received the rite of circumcision. The true children of Abraham are those, whether Jew or Gentile, who demonstrate the same faith as Abraham.

> '. . . he is the father of all who have faith when uncircumcised, and so have righteousness "counted" to them; and at the same time he is the father of the circumcised, provided that they are not merely circumcised, but also follow that path of faith which our father Abraham trod while he was still uncircumcised'. (Romans 4.11b-12)

Faithfulness to the past is not to be seen in slavishly copying the past but in exercising the same kind of faith as those who went before us. Perhaps if we tested our own denominational circumstances against the spirit of our forbears' concerns, rather than duplicating the letter of the way they worked out the gospel for their time, we might more ably walk in the footprints of their faith.

All in Each Place

We need to return continually to the local situation, for example, the town with many churches. It has often been argued that for ecumenism to work, it must work 'at the grassroots'. Perhaps we should say that if ecumenism is to grow it must grow at the grassroots. The metaphors and cliches tumble out: the 'cutting edge', the 'coal face', 'where the action is', 'the real world'. Whatever agreements happen at national or international level, they need to live and bear fruit in the local church where Christians gather for worship and from where they go out in service and witness in the world.

It has been argued that the test of any genuine unity should be the test of fellowship and witness in the local situation. Places, and therefore culture, will differ – but within one place there should be a real expression of common witness and faith. This was affirmed at the third Assembly of the World Council of Churches which met at New Delhi in 1961:

> 'We believe that the unity which is both God's will and his gift to his church is being made visible as **all in each place** who are baptized into Jesus Christ and confess him as Lord and Saviour are brought by the Holy Spirit into one fully committed fellowship, holding the one apostolic faith, preaching the one Gospel, breaking the one bread, joining in common prayer, and having a corporate life reaching out in witness and service to all, and who at the same time are united with the whole Christian fellowship in all places and all ages in such wise that ministry and members are accepted by all, and that all can act and speak together as occasion requires for the tasks to which God calls his people'. [3]

This phrase all in each place does not propose a uniform congregation for each town, but a fellowship, 'holding the one apostolic faith, preaching the one Gospel, breaking the one bread, joining in common prayer, and having a corporate life reaching out in witness and service to all'. This fellowship will need to be *embedded* in the local situation if it is to engage in witness and service to all and if its preaching of the one Gospel is to make sense to those who hear. Nonetheless, it will be 'united with the whole Christian fellowship in all places and all ages'.

Given the present diversity of denominations and the diversity of cultural situations, we need to ask *how* such local and universal unity might be achieved. The answers will be many and various and we must admit that this discussion constitutes a large part of the agenda of the ecumenical movement. How *is* unity to be achieved? Some will say that agreements need to be hammered out at international level so as to enable progress at the grassroots. Others will point to the need for common witness at a national level where churches can unite in a shared mission to the needs of a nation. Others will argue that unity must be experimented with and explored in the local situation if the other levels are to have any meaning. Our understanding of the church will have an influence on our judgement here, but we must recognize that each level is important in order to help the other levels to develop and advance.

One national response to the New Delhi phrase 'all in each place' has been the encouragement in England of *Areas of Ecumenical Experiment*.[4] These were attempts to enable local congregations to live, worship and witness in patterns of unity which vary from place to place. The aim was to act and worship together as far as denominational regulations would allow. In time, some of these regulations have been altered in the light of the experiments. Intermediate *Sponsoring Bodies* were established by the denominations in an attempt to support and learn from these local experiments in unity. After a few years the title of these local experiments was changed to *Local Ecumenical Projects*. The change from *experiment* to *project* was a recognition that the search for unity is a long haul and not the temporary affair that *experiment* might suggest.

However, after twenty years of life, in some cases, we still need to remember the importance of the original title. The idea of experiment is not only for the benefit of the local Christians but for the education and challenging of *national* bodies and the encouragement of further experiments elsewhere. Equally, the experiments have underlined the way in which the local unity, however deeply committed, is limited and sometimes distorted by the regulations and partial concerns of national denominations. On the other side we must recognize that the denominations through the sponsoring bodies are, in the experimental sense, an important 'control'. To place too great an emphasis on the avoidance of law-breaking would be to go against the spirit of experiment. However, there needs to be a questioning voice which ensures that local unity is a unity 'in truth' if it is to be fully a witness to 'the truth of unity'. At the same time, we can see that *international* agreements like the text *Baptism, Eucharist and Ministry* have an enriching and encouraging influence on the local ecumenical situation.

All in each place is thus a challenge to the church at every level. Its call to unity is grounded in the pattern of church life which we find not only reflected but advocated in the New Testament. It reminds us that the search for unity is inspired by a spirit of reconciliation which will include *all* people. It is grounded in concern for discipleship *in* the reality of God's world and is challenged by a concern for mission in the differing circumstances and needs of *each* place.

Here is a practical and Scriptural challenge and invitation to share in the search for unity. It is a challenge which recogizes the measure of unity many Christians experience when they are set free to worship and witness together. But is also leads us on to question those things which continue to make their unity limited and which keep other Christians apart. While some Christians might have achieved a measure of unity in practice, we still need to enquire as to how that is possible. At the same time we need to explore the *basis* for such unity in the hope that it might provide clues to the way in which unity might be found elsewhere. Is there a common faith which unites Christians? Is there sufficient agreement about what Christians believe to talk meaningfully about *One Faith*, despite the diversity which both enriches and divides the church?

Confessing One Faith
Is it possible to speak of Christians 'holding the one apostolic faith'? The New Delhi statement did not claim that all Christians shared this faith, but that the unity of the church was made visible when the various things mentioned in that text, including this phrase, were realised in the local situation. While it is possible for Christians to do many things together, do not denominational and cultural differences suggest that there is *not* a common faith? The answer of course depends in part on how we define our terms. If we mean *full* agreement on every matter of doctrine, then our answer will have to be in the negative. However, there would be many Christians from many denominations who would claim that they are in agreement over *essentials*.

The difficulty then shifts to what we mean by *essentials*. It was a feature of nineteenth century liberal Protestantism to try and distil the *essence of Christianity*.[5] The result was usually a reduced gospel which was intelligible to liberal intellectuals but which no longer seemed to be good news.

A more hopeful concept is the idea that there is a *hierarchy of truths* within the Christian faith. This idea is affirmed in the decree on ecumenism of the Second Vatican Council.[6] This principle provides a method whereby theologians can distinguish between those doctrines which are *fundamental* to Christianity and other doctrines which are built upon those fundamentals. The claim is made that Christians agree about fundamentals and only disagree about the secondary doctrines. This principle has the advantage of making sense both of the recognition of each others' faith and of that shared Faith which Christians discover when they get together at the local level for worship, discussion and service. But is the principle one which will stand up to scrutiny? *Are* Christians agreed about fundamentals?

This question has become the basis of an important programme of the Faith and Order Commission of the World Council of Churches. The commission not only embraces the streams of Protestantism and Orthodoxy within the World Council, but also the Roman Catholic Church. While engaged on other programmes dealing with convergence in *Baptism, Eucharist and Ministry* and *The Unity of the Church and the Renewal of Human Community*, it is working on a long-term programme with the title: *'Towards the Common Expression of the Apostolic Faith Today'*. The sixth Assembly of the World Council of Churches meeting in Vancouver in 1983 endorsed the work already undertaken by the Faith and Order Commission and then the report said:

> *'. . . it has become clear that any common attempts by the churches to express the faith which unites all contemporary churches and all believers of all ages with the apostolic church would need to be conceived along three lines: first, a common* **recognition** *of the apostolic faith as expressed in creeds of the undivided church such as the Apostolic Symbol*[7] *and especially the Nicene Creed: second, a common* **explication** *of the faith so recognized in terms understandable today; and third, a common* **confession** *by the churches today of that same apostolic faith in relation to contemporary challenges to the Gospel.'*[8]

The creed which has been chosen as the basis for the attempt to express a common faith is the *Nicene Creed*.[9] It has been chosen for a number of reasons. First, it is widely used in Orthodox, Roman Catholic and Anglican worship as a means of expressing the Faith in worship. Secondly, it also features in some of the confessions of faith of the Reformation, where it is acknowledged as the basis of faith before the respective documents go on to affirm additional concerns. Thirdly, it dates from the time of the first four Ecumenical Councils of the church.[10] In other words, it is claimed to date from a time when the church was one and undivided.

Our investigations might well make us wary of this latter argument which seems to be based on the *golden age* theory. However, we can make two observations. First, it is not only history but perceptions of history which are important in acknowledging the historic significance of such a document as the Nicene Creed. If present-day churches are each able to trace their identity to that period of the story then that in itself gives the creed a particular status as the confession document of a shared history. Secondly, in the sense that the Ecumenical Councils of Nicea (AD 325) and Constantinople (AD 381) were representative of the whole church in the known world the creed can rightly claim to be the product of an undivided church. This does not mean that there were no disagreements or differences. The councils were called in a climate of controversy to define the Faith in the face of threatening heresy. But that credal expression of the Faith was representative of those who were in communion with each other at the time. [11]

Some churches have reservations about the use of the Nicene Creed, but, before we can comment on these, we need to see how the Nicene Creed is to be used in the search for a common expression of the apostolic faith today.

> 'Using the Nicene Constantinopolitan Creed as a methodoligical tool, the churches are asked to go back through the words of the Creed to the normative witness of Holy Scripture and to re-capture the faith of the Bible reflected in the Creed'. [12]

There are three parts to the programme.

First, the churches are called to *recognize* the apostolic faith as expressed in the Nicene Creed. This recognition is both an acceptance of the creed itself as a basic statement of faith and a means of relating the creed to the various ways in which the churches have expressed their faith. So the recognition process is about using the creed to explain the beliefs of one church to another. This will have the double benefit of enabling a church to relate its testimony to a common confession and enabling other churches to recognize the shared faith in the particular expression of the church concerned.

Secondly, the churches are called to a common *explication*. Together, the churches are called to make sense of the creed in the language of today and with a view to the relevance of the doctrines of the creed and the needs of today. For example, the creed confesses *one God*. What does that mean for the modern tendencies to make absolute the political ideologies and personal ambitions of our age? What does the confession of one God who created all things mean for a human community torn apart by poverty, militarism and racism? [13]

Thirdly, the churches are called to make a common *confession* of the apostolic faith today. As a step along this path contemporary confessions of faith from around the world have been gathered together in a series of books. [14] Each represents an attempt to give expression to the common faith in particular situations. As we would expect, there is great diversity. Eventually an attempt will be made at a *common* contemporary confession of faith which will complement but not replace the historic creeds. The task is for the future, but we must recognize its importance both as an act of witness for the world and as a discovering of a shared identity on the part of the Christian community.

However, there are some churches who have never used formal creeds either in worship or as a doctrinal statement of faith. These traditions inevitably express concern at the direction of the programme. They are called to reconsider their reservations 'for the sake of unity'. Such a request might seem unfair, but we must note the sensitivity with which the programme has been planned. Churches are not asked to adopt the creed as a test of faith or to begin using it regularly in worship. Rather, the creed is to be seen as a tool to enable Christians to recognize together a common Faith. The use of the creed in this way has been explained as a 'grid through which the believer could interpret both the ampler witness of Scripture and the church and also his own religious stance'.[15]

To this we might add that an awareness of the historical setting of the creed might help some to overcome their reservations. The ecclesiastical, social and political context in which the creed was formulated was a concrete situation which demanded a particular expression of the gospel. While recognizing the creed as in some sense normative, the status we give it is inevitably controlled by an awareness of this setting. We saw in our study of the New Testament that there is no such thing as a pure, unapplied expression of the Gospel. Every expression of the Faith will be embedded in a particular situation. The creed is no different from Scripture in that respect. If it is normative, then it can only be normative in the way that the example of Abraham is normative. To be a child of Abraham means displaying the kind of faith that Abraham showed. Similarly, to recognize the apostolic faith in the Nicene Creed means undertaking the task of confessing the faith as the Ecumenical Councils did. It means using their confessions as a tool, but is also means making a *shared* confession today – making a confession so that the world might believe.[16] The *Statement to the Churches* of the WCC Faith and Order Plenary Commission held in Budapest in 1989 commented on the task of seeking a common confession of faith:

> 'While recognizing the difficulty of the task, the pain of our divided lives is urging us to express humbly our willingness to undertake the demanding search for a common expression of faith. We do this in the hope that from God's hand we shall receive together the gift of unity in Christ through the power of the Holy Spirit and be renewed in the task of witnessing to that unity in the world.'[17]

All this talk has been about the *use* of the creed rather than its *content*. The heart of confession is the revelation of the triune God in Jesus Christ, who, for our salvation, became incarnate as a human being and was crucified and raised. All our discussions about what might unite Christians in their diversity must lead to this point – the recognition of Jesus Christ as the author and finisher of our faith.

Confessing One Lord

The various expressions of the Gospel in the New Testament have one thing in common. They identify the saving reality of their faith, by which they are brought close to God, with Jesus of Nazareth who was crucified and is now raised. The boundaries which are set around a legitimate diversity are also linked to this centre. If local expressions of the Faith cease to confess the centrality of Jesus for salvation and faith in God then they have crossed a boundary. Similarly, if Christians behave in such a way as to contradict the love of God in Christ then again they have crossed a boundary.

Both the creeds and the Scriptures point to Jesus Christ. Our knowledge of God is through the Word made flesh in him. We are able to recognize the activity of God in the world through his Spirit by comparing what we see now with what we have seen in Jesus. Jesus Christ is both at the centre and at the boundary of Christian identity. Orthodox Christian teaching would say that there is more of God than we see in Jesus but we can only recognize God in his fulness by the perspective of what has been revealed in Christ.

> 'It was there from the beginning; we have heard it; we have seen it with our own eyes; we looked upon it, and felt it with our own hands: our theme is the Word which gives life. This life was made visible; we have seen it and bear our testimony; we declare to you the eternal life which was with the Father and was made visible to us. It is this which we have seen and heard that we declare to you also, in order that you may share with us in a common life, that life which we share with the Father and his Son Jesus Christ.' (1 John 1.1-3)

Jurgen Moltmann comments on the words of the creed *one holy, catholic and apostolic church.* Because,

> 'the church acquires its existence through the activity of Christ, then her character-istics, too, are characteristics of Christ's activity first of all. The acknowledgement of the 'one, holy, catholic and apostolic church' is acknowledgement of the uniting, sanctifying, comprehensive and commissioning lordship of Christ'. [18]

The *oneness* of the church is to be seen in Christ's gathering of believers by his Spirit. The *holiness* of the church is the holiness of the Christ who acts for sinners. The *catholicity* of the church is the limitless lordship of Christ, for where Christ rules, there is the church. The *apostolic* character of the church is to be seen within the framework of the mission of Christ and the Spirit. These characteristics are both present realities and future hopes and it is to bear witness and give expression to these that the church exists. Thus the whole church only has meaning in and under Christ.

It is therefore possible to speak of Christ as giving the church its identity. As such we have an identity which transcends denominational and party boundaries, even though it will always have to find expression in specific human institutions and persons. Here is not only the common identity of the Christian church, but *one Lord* to be confessed, trusted and followed.

If we ask whether there is a basic unity which encompasses Christians in their diversity and division we must reply that it is a unity 'in Christ'. Without him we are nothing. That does not mean that as human beings we cease to count, but that as a church we would cease to have meaning. Here is the strongest and gentlest argument of all in the cause of ecumenism. *We have one Lord Jesus Christ and in him we are one.* In him God loves us and saves us. In him God gives us hope. In him God calls us to follow.

Before asking about the path of discipleship together, and where it might lead, we need to pursue our enquiry into unity and diversity from a quite different angle. Having explored diversity in the New Testament and the basis for unity in the Lordship of Christ, we need to examine the contribution of *theological method* to our debate. The way we talk about God and the methods we use to express our faith have a contribution to make in our search to understand the relationship of unity to diversity.

Notes

1. In our local town there may be different cultures, due to migration, and this may well mean different congregations formed around different cultural concerns and expressions. On the other hand, there will be occasions when factors may lead to a sharing of different cultures in a multi-lingual, multi-cultural sharing. While this is to be prized as a rich example of communion, it must be recognized that the nature of our humanity leads us to establish different congregations in different cultural situations.

2. The pattern of a single bishop as the focus of unity was widespread by the middle of the second century. Its origins are usually discerned in the epistles of Ignatius of Antioch which are dated at the beginning of the second century, at the close of the New Testament period. See F. Hawkins, 'The Tradition of Ordination in the Second century to the time of Hippolytus' in 'The Study of Liturgy' ed. Jones, Wainwright and Yarnold (London) 1978 pp297-306. See also 'Baptism, Ministry and Eucharist' WCC (Geneva) 1982 p24.

3. WCC, 'The New Delhi Report' (London) 1962 p116.

4. The British Faith and Order Conference of 1964 was called in reponse to the challenge of New Delhi. It called on the churches 'to designate *areas of experiment*, at the request of local congregations, or in new towns and housing areas'. At the beginning of 1990 there were over 550 Local Ecumenical Projects in England.

5. See S. Sykes, 'The Identity of Christianity' (London) 1984 esp pp81-238. It is also interesting to note the *adiaphorist* party (from Greek *adiaphora* 'things indifferent') in Sixteenth Century German Protestantism. Melanchthon and others declared certain Catholic practices such as confirmation, extreme unction and the veneration of the saints 'adiaphora' ie. 'matters on which concessions might be made in the interest of peace without prejudice to Protestant doctrine'. In 1577 Article 10 of the Formula of Concord ruled that 'in times of persecution concessions were not to be made, but otherwise ceremonies not commanded or forbidden by Scripture might be altered according to the decisions of

individual Churches'. See F.L. Cross, 'The Oxford Dictionary of the Christian Church', London 1957 p17.

6. Second Vatican Council 'Decree on Ecumenism' paragraph 11. Also Yves Congar, 'Diversity and Communion', ET (London) 1984 pp126-133. At the time of writing, fresh work is being undertaken on this subject by a joint Roman Catholic/WCC group.

7. ie. *The Apostles' Creed.*

8. 'Gathered for Life: Report of the sixth Assembly of the WCC, Vancouver 1983', ed. David Gill (Geneva) 1983 p48. The early stages of this project included the collecting of confessions of faith from around the world: see Faith and Order papers 104, 120, 123, 126 and 'Sharing in One Hope'. Faith and Order Paper 140 is the study document, 'Confessing One Faith: Towards an ecumenical explication of the Apostolic Faith as expressed in the Nicene-Constantinopolitan Creed (381)'.

9. The creed which we today call *The Nicene Creed* is more adquately named 'The Nicene-Constantinopolitan Creed' as it is the creed from the first Ecumenical Council at Nicea in 325, possibly amplified in 381 at the Council of Constantinople and affirmed at the Council of Chalcedon in 451. It probably originated as the baptismal creed of the church in Jerusalem, with certain additions, and soon afterwards began to be included as a confession of faith in eucharistic liturgies of East and West. However, the inclusion of the 'Filioque Clause' (the Spirit proceeds from the Father *and the Son*) was gradually added in the western use of the creed and was one of the causes of the split between east and west in the eleventh century. This clause is still a cause of stumbling today and the version of the creed in the Faith and Order programme is the original text of 381 which does not include the words 'and the Son'.

10. The term *Ecumenical Council* comes from the Greek *oikoumene*, 'the whole inhabited earth' – see chapter two. Such a council is an assembly of bishops and other church representatives from the whole (known) world whose decisions are seen as binding on the church. Their authority is variously understood but always it is under the authority of Scripture and the full recognition of a council has been through its reception by the church. Some traditions will wish to see in the Councils the *authentic* interpretation of Scripture, especially when there is disagreement about its interpretation. Because of the Great Schism between East and West of 1054 the Eastern churches do not recognize the 14 councils of the Roman Catholic Church called after that time, as they are not comprehensively representative. There is widespread recognition, including some of the churches of the Reformation, of the first four councils. These were Nicea I (325), Constantinople I (381), Ephesus (431), Chalcedon (451). Recent suggestions have been made for regarding the first four councils as a basis for doctrinal agreement between the churches today.

11. For arguments in favour of the use of the Nicene Creed see M. Kinnamon ed. 'Towards Visible Unity: Study papers and reports of the Commission on Faith and Order, Lima 1982' (Geneva) 1982 pp32-36. See also the introduction in J. Lochman, 'The Faith We Confess' (Philadelphia) 1984.

12. Mary Tanner, 'Where are we? Where are we going? The work of Faith and Order in the 1980's' in J.H.Y. Briggs, ed. 'Faith, Heritage and Witness: A supplement to the Baptist Quarterly published in honour of Dr W.M.S. West', Baptist Historical Society, 1987, p54.

13. See 'Towards Visible Unity' pp37-39.

14. 'Confessing our Faith around the world' vols 1-4, published by the WCC.

15. G. Wainwright, 'Doxology: A systematic theology' (London) 1980 p192.

16. For further discussion of the problems of recognizing the Nicene Creed see Thomas F. Best, ed. 'Faith and Renewal: Reports and Documents of the Commission on Faith and Order, Stavanger 1985' (Geneva) 1986, pp160-162. It is possible to make a distinction between *one creed* and *many confessions*. Athanasius commented after Nicea that no one was using the Nicene Creed, but the various regions were continuing to use their own local confessions. Many creeds continued to be produced in the Western Church between the fourth and ninth centuries. The Nicene Creed became 'universal' in the Eastern Churches in 520AD after its incorporation into the liturgy by the non Chalcedonians (501) and the Chalcedonians (520) as an attempt to demonstrate who really was orthodox. In the West, the Apostles Creed became universal by edict of Charlemagne in about 800AD so that the clergy should at least know the Apostle's Creed as a criterion of their education. We must therefore be cautious when we try to speak of a *universal* creed.

17. Available at time of writing in a duplicated form but to be made available in the official account of the proceedings and published by the World Council of Churches.

18. Jurgen Moltmann, 'The Church in the Power of the Spirit' ET (London) 1977 p338.

Chapter Six

TRUTH IN TENSION

The Ecumenical Centre in Geneva is the headquarters of the World Council of Churches, as well as a number of other international church organizations. A visitor to the centre cannot fail to notice the rich variety of people who work in and visit that place. People from different continents work side by side, different languages buzz around the dining room.

As well as the rich human variety, a visitor will notice in the chapel and around the building a number of works of art, which reflect both different church traditions and different parts of the world. Perhaps we should not call these items 'works of art' because they are often religious objects which have been devoutly crafted in an attempt to help people to worship.

On climbing the main stairs the visitor will find on the landing a picture painted in a very simple way, but gorgeously coloured and decorated with gold. This picture is not sumptuously produced in order to excite our sense of how valuable it must be, but because the subject it depicts is such a sublime one that no medium but the best could possibly be good enough. The glory of the gold is to direct our thoughts, and then our hearts, to an awareness of the glory of God, for the picture is an icon and the subject is the Trinity.

We might well wonder how an artist could dare to represent that which theologians have argued about, and mystics wrestled with, since the early years of the church. The artist dares to attempt such a thing because he or she has brought a God-given gift to the great task of helping others to mediate on the glory of God. The icon's purpose is to aid worship and devotion, not to provide a complete picture of God. The Council of Constantinople (AD 867) declared: 'That which the book (the Bible) tells us in words, the icon announces to us in colour and makes present to us.' The icon seeks to approach the mystery of God and to help others to approach that mystery. Yet, despite its glories and the wonderful way that the Spirit inspired the artist and inspires those who come prayerfully before it, the icon has its limits just as does every approach to God. Some theologians and some councils of the church have tended to emphasize one aspect of God at the expense of other aspects, so this is the case with the icon, which, on one panel, offers one picture.

Through a Glass Darkly

The doctrine of the Trinity is an attempt to acknowledge that God has fully revealed himself as the Creator *and* as a human being *and* as the life-giving

Spirit at work in the world. At the same time it wishes to hold on to the belief that these are not three separate gods but *one* God. So the time-honoured phrase 'three in one and one in three' is not so much an attempt to nail God down to a set of words, as to hold within the paradox of human language the vision of God as greater than anything we can imagine, but nonetheless revealed to us in a series of ways we can begin to understand. But the very tension within a paradox leads each of us to emphasize the pull of one side more than another. So some theologians have stressed the unity and oneness of God while others have stressed the threeness.

The icon in Geneva is firmly rooted in the tradition of those who have found more sense in stressing the threeness of God's revelation. It is a copy of the famous fifteenth century icon painted by Andrei Rublev which portrays the three visitors who came to Abraham and Sarah at Mamre (Genesis chapter 18). There has long been a tradition within the church which has seen the threeness of God reflected in that ancient story. The picture shows three human images for, it is argued, if humanity has been created in the image and likeness of God then we can only portray the three Persons of the Trinity as three human persons. Henri Nouwen has spoken of this icon as an invitation to live in 'the house of love'. He writes:

> 'From within this holy circle this house of love, the mystery of God is revealed to us . . . It is the mystery of hospitality expressed not only in Abraham's and Sarah's welcome of the three angels, but also in God's welcome of the aged couple into the joy of the covenant through an heir.' [1]

Eastern theology has tended to emphasize the threeness of God which is expressed in the icon. From this view of God there may follow the argument which runs like this. The Persons of the Trinity are a supreme example of how several persons are bound together by love in such a way that they are ultimately not three but one. If this is our understanding of God, then we must seek such a reality for the life of the world and the life of the church. In the Fourth Gospel Jesus prays for his disciples and those who become believers as a result of their preaching:

> 'May they all be one; as you Father, are in me, and I in you, so also may they be in us, that the world may believe that you sent me.' (John 17.21)

'Bind us together Lord, Bind us together with cords that cannot be broken' is a modern hymn which expresses the prayer of the church that the People of God be not only trinitarian in their doctrine but also in their life in the Spirit.

This perspective on the Trinity as bound by love has often been used as a means of inspiring love, and consequently unity, in the church. But there is another way in which the doctrine of the Trinity can help us in our reflections on unity. This further reflection begins with the very *shape* of the doctrine and gains inspiration from the nature of *paradox* and the liveliness of *tension*.

If we start with the affirmation that God is one, we stand firmly within the biblical tradition. But as we read the Bible we are led to see that God has shown himself to us in a number of *different* ways.

God has revealed himself to us as *Creator*, the Lord who brings order out of chaos, who breathes life into the dust of the earth and who receives the praise of the whole creation.

But God has also revealed himself as a *human being*. Karl Barth pointed out that the doctrine of the Trinity began when Christians wanted to call Jesus *Lord*, the word which was used for God in the Greek Old Testament. It was an awareness that here we encountered God in a unique way that provided the church with the data which somehow had to be reconciled with the belief in *one* God inherited from the Old Testament. [2]

There was also an awareness that God was active in the world through his *Spirit*. In the transformation of lives, in the inspiration and guiding of the apostles, Christians saw the Spirit of God at work. The belief that this was no delegated activity but God himself, made them face the problem as to how this could be reconciled to belief in one God.

It was no good trying to argue that these were three stages in the history of the world. It couldn't be argued that the Father was the God of the Old Testament, Jesus the God of the Gospels and the Spirit the God of the church. While an initial reading of the Bible might tempt some to walk down that path, a further reading would show it to be a dead end. The Spirit is at work in the story of creation in the first chapter of Genesis; the Spirit inspires many of the leaders and prophets of Israel; [3] Ezekiel sees the Spirit as the activity of God breathing new life into a lifeless nation. [4] The Spirit is involved in the birth of Jesus, [5] present at his baptism [6] and is seen as active throughout his ministry. While one could argue that the birth of Jesus is the starting point of a new era, the Fourth Gospel claims that is it the eternal Word who is made flesh in this man. [7] Thus mainstream Christian theology has claimed that God has revealed himself as Father, Son and Spirit – and that Father, Son and Spirit are all active in creation, redemption and sanctification. [8]

However we try to make sense of the doctrine of the Trinity, we are left with a simple fact. We have two statements about God which seem if not to conflict with each other, at least to stand in tension. On the one hand, we claim that God is the Creator, that he is a Son and that he is Spirit. On the other hand we confess that he is these three persons *at the same time*, that he is *one*.

Now what one person calls *paradox* another calls *contradiction*, but before we dismiss all this as another example of theological juggling, we will do well to remember two things.

First, *any* theological statement is a human statement and therefore unlikely to be an adequate statement about God. Even when Christians talk about revealed truth, we have to recognize that, in order to be understandable to human beings, such truth cannot be more than a human mind can cope with and therefore it will still be an inadequate statement about God. We affirm that the Old Testament law was God-given, yet, in the light of Christ, Christians would want to see it as at least incomplete. This is not arrogance but a recognition of our human limitation and that even God must take account of this in his dealing with us. Like the icon of the Trinity, any theological statement will be a failure, albeit a glorious failure. This acceptance of limitation doesn't throw truth out of the window, because all human truth is an attempt to approach reality. We have to make judgements as to whether each attempt is moving towards or moving away from reality.

This recognition of the limitations of human language is nothing new. In the fourth century Hilary of Poitiers invited his readers to,

> 'confess by our silence that words cannot describe Him; let sense admit that it is foiled in the attempt to apprehend and that reason is foiled in the attempt to define'. [9]

He concluded that our best theological endeavours are merely,

> 'an acknowledgement of His glory, a hint of our meaning, a sketch of our thoughts; but speech is powerless to tell us what God is, words cannot express the reality'. [10]

In the eighth century John of Damascus wrote,

> 'God then is infinite and incomprehensible and all that is comprehensible about Him is his infinity and incomprehensibility.' [11]

All this enables us to guard against an insidious form of idolatry. The Bible condemns the worship of human-made images. Just as many people need visual images – a cross, a face, a light – to help them to worship, so many of us need words and theological statements to help us to conceive of God at all. *Idolatry begins when the aids to worship become the object of worship, whether they be statues or sentences.* Icons and words should point us beyond themselves towards God. Christians in the Protestant tradition have often pointed the finger at the devotional practices of other Christians and, in their use of statues and images, accused them of idolatry – while at the same time idolatrously guarding statements of faith which are formulated by human beings and limited to what human beings can understand.

Secondly, human talk about God is relative to our culture, experience, understanding and inclination. Just as an artist will work within the limitations of a particular medium – stone, paint, music – so the person thinking about God constructs and develops images of God which use the raw materials to hand. These will include Scripture and tradition, but we must not under-estimate the influence of cultural values, patterns of thought and pastoral concerns. We should not regret these influences, for if theology is to be relevant to the needs of actual people it will need to be formed by their concerns as well as by the main features of the Gospel. As we have already observed, the very idea of *Gospel* – good news – suggests a relevance of content and presentation to a particular people in a particular situation which involves the use of contemporary thought forms as well as language. You cannot have 'news' in a vacuum. Information has to be relevant to a particular audience for it to become news. This leads to a recognition that other Christians, living in different circumstances, will arrive at different perceptions of God. It may only be a difference of emphasis, or there may seem to be a more fundamental tension. Encounter with other Christians from other church traditions or other continents will lead us into a very trinitarian position of wanting to say different things about God, yet wanting to hold these different statements in tension.

Facets of Understanding

This is not unique to Christian thought about God. In any area of knowledge and enquiry where we are approaching something that is not easily explained, we tend to hold 'contradictory' statements in tension. Physicists speak of light as rays travelling in a straight line. But they also speak of light as travelling in waves. Now these two pictures are both held to be true at the same time.

In the cubist portrait of a person's face you might find both a square, front view *and* a profile view of an eye and a nose. The cubists were attempting to paint a person from a number of different angles *at the same time*. If you claim that this is not very realistic because when we look at someone in the flesh we only see them from one angle, then we have to acknowledge that one angle is not the whole person, and that it is sometimes good to be reminded of that fact. It is also a valid goal for an artist to try to show us more of reality than we can normally see.

These observations about the limitations of language and perception lead us back to the doctrine of the Trinity. While it may not lead us into the heart of the mystery, this discussion may help us to see that there *is* a mystery and how we can live with it.

We are reminded that there are limits to what we can achieve in attempting to talk about God and that often our own insights can be enriched by holding them alongside the insights of others. From the human perspective this might, at times, lead to the embracing of an apparent contradiction, but, like the cubist painting, it might be an attempt to approach God from two or more directions at the same time.

Alternatively, we could think of two maps of the same country. One map shows the relief features – the rivers, mountains and valleys – while the other map shows the geological formations which underlie that landscape. These two maps will have certain features in common – the coastline or national boundary, for example – but they will also appear very different. Each map, if accurate, can be said to be a true map of the country. The objection might be made that a map does not claim to be the only true representation of a geographical area, and that we would normally expect several maps to be complementary. However, it is possible to claim that in some sense we must see our images of God and our understanding of his purposes in a similar way.

We could develop this illustration further. For example, until the recent exploration of space and the photographing of the continents from orbiting spacecraft, no-one had seen a country as portrayed on a map – the lines of the map would have been pieced together by the efforts, observation and measuring of many different people over many years. We would do well to remember that the New Testament points out that no-one has ever seen God. Our theological maps are dependent on piecing together the experience and testimony of those who have encountered him at work in their lives: testimony handed down from the past and testimony shared in the present. It is encouraging to remember that when we first saw those photographs from space they were remarkably like the maps which we already had.

All this talk of maps and icons might seem a very long-winded way of stating the belief that we need to accept other people's insights. But I believe the point is so important that we must not miss it, especially as it is under threat in the modern world. We live in a world where fundamentalist religion wants the truth tied up in packaged propositions. The political and religious climate is often one of people wanting hard, clear statements of the way things are. Anyone who pleads for the exercising of caution or who wishes to embrace more than one position is labelled a 'woolly liberal'. From a position of openness it is often difficult to discuss meaningfully with a person who has a closed system of belief. This is why we need a theological basis for openness – a commitment to dialogue and mutual dependence which is based on our belief in the greatness and glory of God, the limitations of all human endeavour and the biblical challenge to live a life of faith.

An Ecumenical Theology

Here is the heart of ecumenical theology – it is based on these three things. There is first an awareness of the *greatness of God* which transcends any human attempt to describe him, any human formulation or institution. There is then the awareness of our own *creatureliness* as well as our own sin, which limits and distorts all we attempt. Finally, there is the glorious gospel which tells us that all this does not matter, for *God beckons us to live lives which reach out in faith* to he who comes close to us in Christ and through his Spirit. This life of faith involves both a faith which trusts in the mercy of God and a faith which leads us to reach out to each other. Jesus said, 'Blessed are the poor'. An awareness of our poverty enables us to be open to and reach out for the riches of God. Thus our creaturely limitation is the opportunity for faith in God and the seeking out of our fellow human beings. An awareness that my own denomination is so limited pushes me to seek the enriching fellowship of other Christians. And it is there that I encounter afresh the glory of God.

This is not a claim that it doesn't matter what Christians believe, nor should we seek a church of the lowest common denominator. Ecumenism is not about throwing all our treasures into a melting pot so that we end up with a uniform church. What is being claimed is that we each bring the treasures and insights entrusted to us down the ages, and lay them all before the altar of God's compassion. *We need to hold truths in tension.* Just as we believe in God as Father, Son and Spirit, yet one God, so we hold in tension our insights about God's purposes for humanity, our understanding of the church and our mission in the world.

If such a vision appears confusing or threatening, then we must remember that we are not called to certainty, but to a life of faith. There are many parts of the Christian church which would want to make absolute and exclusive claims about their view of Christianity and the church. Such claims betray a less than Christian view of the truth. If this seems particularly harsh then here are three reasons for such a judgement.

First, we must state that *only God is absolute.* Any human set of words will remain a human set of words and therefore limited by our creatureliness. To make absolute claims for dogmas and creeds is just as idolatrous as worshipping wood or stone. Words are the product of human creativity just as much as more conventional idols. Our awareness of the glory of God compels us to recognize that we are creatures and that all we do is within the limitations of this world. God is the Creator and therefore beyond our loftiest imaginings. Hilary again:

> 'Our confession of God fails through the defects of language; the best combi-nation of words we can devise cannot indicate the reality and the greatness of God . . . We must believe, must apprehend, must worship; and such acts of devotion must stand in lieu of definition.' [12]

Secondly, a claim to absolute truth closes the possibility of being led into more truth. This is *a denial of the Holy Spirit* and a closing of our minds to the activity of God in the present as well as the past. Jesus said that the Spirit would lead us into all truth – we must not close our minds to that promise. Christians have often described their faith as *a pilgrimage,* but as such it must always be seen as a journey which does not end in this life. In 1620 Pastor John Robinson addressed the Pilgrim Fathers before they left for the New World and charged them to be open to what God had still to say to them. For he was confident that 'the Lord had more truth and light yet to break forth out of his holy word'.[13]

Thirdly, *we are called to a life of faith.* This does not so much mean giving assent to the absolute claims of *The Faith,* as living a life which is open to God's promises and dependent on his grace. Absolute dogmas don't require faith because they offer certainty, a mechanical relationship to the promises of God rather than a relationship of trust and hope. Paul writes,

> '*It was with this hope that we were saved. Now to see something is no longer to hope: why hope for what is already seen?*' *(Romans 8.24)*

These arguments are not new. The unknown prophet whom we call Second Isaiah, preaching to the exiles in Babylon, was concerned to make the people ready so that they might respond to God's saving action when it offered them the opportunity to return to the promised land. They had developed a ghetto mentality and had stopped expecting God to act any more. He was a God of the past, to be offered their religious duty but not their breathless expectation. The prophet reminded the exiles that their God was not some quaint memory to be unrolled with the Sabbath scrolls but the Creator of the universe who unrolls the heavens and stretches out the sky like a curtain. It is this prophet who was so withering in his condemnation of idolatry – his God was too big for the fumbling attempts of even the best craftsmen. His hearers were happy bemoaning their fate but were not prepared to trust God. Yet the prophet told them that the God who brought their ancestors out of slavery in Egypt and through the dangers of the Red Sea and the desert would again bring his people from exile to the land which was the symbol of all his promises, as well as the arena of his saving actions.

Just as it was a vision of the greatness of God the Creator, and faith in the power of his promises of salvation, which provided the power of the preaching of Second Isaiah, so it is these things which must provide the basis and the framework for an ecumenical theology. Just as Christian worship begins with praise, so our feeble attempts to offer God the devotion of our struggling minds must begin with adoration. As a theology student I spent much of my reading time in search of a guru, a theologian with whom I could wholly agree. As a teenager I had left behind a biblical fundamentalism and went in search of a replacement ideology, a system within which I could feel safe and which would provide me with at least a derivative identity. I rummaged around the Twentieth Century tomes of Barth and Bultmann, of Tillich and Moltmann and Pannenberg, but I thank God that I never found such a theologian or such a system. This doesn't mean that we are not to learn from others – quite the opposite – but we treat them as fellow pilgrims on the way. We learn from their experience and are enriched by their insights, but we make none of them our idols.

The Stretching of Language

When it was suggested that two different maps of the same geographical area could complement each other, the claim was made that we could see our images of God in a similar way. The very awareness that there are limits both to human language and human understanding has led people to attempt the impossible. *Language has been stretched and transformed in an attempt to explore the reality of God.* One way in which this has been done has been the qualifying of what we say so that we can recognize its limitations. For example, we may speak about a 'personal' God, but we have also to say that he is not the same as a human person, rather, that he is 'at least personal'. If human personality is the highest category in our experience, then it is right that we should use it to talk about God; but we still have to qualify the way in which we use the words – they are still stretched beyond their normal meaning.

There are two other, but related, ways in which we stretch language in talking about God. One is the use of different pictures, several of which may be affirmed at the same time. God as judge, father, breath of life, brother – the very fact that we can use several of these titles in the same breath is a recognition that none of them adequately or exhaustively defines or expresses the mystery of God. Their very co-existence relativizes each picture so that it is seen as a pointer to God, or a facet of his glory, but most definitely not the whole picture.

The other way in which language is stretched is in the use of *paradox* or *dialectic*. The difference between this and the method just outlined is that paradox holds within a single statement or claim the tension of two statements which seem to contradict each other – *truth in tension*. So we might say that God is both knowable and incomprehensible. He has revealed himself in Christ and continues to reveal himself in the experience of believers – yet our knowledge of him is indirect, mediated by the world and the events in the world. Emil Brunner has written,

> '*Like a rod in water God's Word is broken in the element of the world; just as Christ could only reveal the glory of God through the form of a servant, so all speech concerning God, if in the sense of this revelation, is necessarily 'paradoxical'. It is only by means of the contradiction between two ideas – God and man, grace and responsibility, holiness and love – that we can apprehend the contradictory truth that the eternal God enters time, or that the sinful man is declared just.*'[14]

Brunner, Barth and others formed a group of theologians in the early part of this century who were known as exponents of 'Dialectical Theology' and they sought to safeguard the glory of God and the mysteries of the faith by speaking in paradoxes. More recently, John Macquarrie has presented a historical survey which has demonstrated the use of paradox as a strand running through the work of many thinkers down the centuries. Often they were people outside the theological establishment of their time but they could be seen as prophets who sought to safeguard the faith by standing over against the easy domestication of God by containment in systems and exclusive ideologies. He writes,

> 'When I speak of 'dialectical theism', I am not thinking of some weak compromise. 'Dialectic' is to be understood in the strong sense of the clash of opposites; for instance, God is not half transcendent and half immanent, but wholly transcendent (ie. high above us) and wholly immanent (ie. close to us). This may sound like a contradiction. It is so in terms of the logic of the finite, but not of the logic of the infinite.' [15]

Macquarrie identifies a number of dialectic tensions which enable us to have a richer appreciation of the nature of God. His second tension is of particular interest for our present discussion:

> 'The second dialectical opposition in God is that between the one and the many. God is the unity holding all things together and without which there would be chaos. But this is not a barren undifferentiated unity. God is also the fullness of being, and embraces within himself all the richness of being.' [16]

Perhaps we are able to see a tension not betwen unity and diversity but between unity and fullness. This fullness is a rich variety rather than a monochrome sameness. It may be that this approach to the mystery of God will provide us with a way of understanding the natural tensions within the community of the church. A word like fullness may provide a better way of understanding the converse of unity than the word diversity. The world fullness may also lead us to the relationship between diversity and communion.

Be that as it may, the claim made at this point is that just as these theologians can use the idea of dialectic and paradox to help human language and thought approach the glory of God, so we can see the alternative traditions of the church as the dialectic treasures which help rather than hinder us. It has long been claimed that we should rejoice in the variety of the church rather than attempt some monolithic, transnational organization where everyone looks the same. Truth is not something that we can possess, only something that we can recognize, and that recognition is not going to be complete this side of the pearly gates. Therefore, it makes sense to talk about our relationships with each other and the sharing of insights as the relationship of not strangers but pilgrims.

We should rejoice in the dialectic of those Christians who stress that the church is local and those who stress that it is universal. We should rejoice in the splendour of the sung Eucharist and the majesty of the Quaker silence. We should rejoice in the personal leadership of bishops and the fellowship of councils.

We have that variety now. But what makes that variety sinful is that the existence of separate denominations and churches implies exclusive claims which make these churches idolatrous.[17] *Each church has existed as though it were the only true church and thus it has been closed to the truth in others as well as the greater truth, which is only apprehended in the tension between truths.* Only when these churches go in search of unity are they beginning to tackle the sinfulness of the past. But to recognize sin is not to dissolve it. We must seek both the forgiveness of God and the forgiveness of each other as a first step along the road of reconciliation.

So we can begin to construct an ecumenical theology which is founded on the greatness of God, the awareness of our own limitations as finite and sinful creatures, and the invitation of the life-giving Spirit to follow Christ and live a life of faith. This faith is not so much doctrinal assent as an *openness of being* which searches out the glory and refuses to capture it in a single set of words or concepts.

Here is the framework which enables us to provide theological justification for what some would see as benighted woolliness. This framework enables us to discover the truth in others without denying the truth we have already found for ourselves, and it does so without the betrayal of integrity or logic. Here is a way of talking about God and his purpose which has in-built reminders that what we say about him can only point us in a direction.

If we are to use such a framework for our understanding of truth then we need to ask what the implications might be for the life of the Church. If the diversity of the church is a reminder of the greatness of God then what does this mean in the search for unity? How is the principle of *truth in tension* to work out between churches and traditions? If variety is important, why do we need to seek a visible, corporate unity at all? The search for unity takes a lot of time and effort – shouldn't we invest that time and effort in mission rather than tinkering with the ecclesiastical machine? And is it fair, amidst such variety, to talk about *the will of God* – and if it is, what is it?

Notes

1. Henri J.M. Nouwen, 'Behold the Beauty of the Lord: Praying with Icons' (Notre Dame) 1987 p23.

2. Karl Barth, 'Church Dogmatics I.1.' ET (Edinburgh) 1936 p458.

3. eg. Isaiah 61.1.

4. Ezekiel 37.1-14 and Joel 2.28-29.

5. Matthew 1.18,20; Luke 1.35.

6. Matthew 3.16, Mark 1.10, Luke 3.22. See also Luke 3.16 and John 1.32-34.

7. 1.14.

8. One emphasis within theology has been so-called 'Economic Trinitarianism'. (The Greek *oikonomia* = 'house management' and, by extension, God's

ruling of the cosmos and therefore his relationship with creation.) This view claims that we perceive God's diversity in revelation but that we should not read back into his essence that which has been necessary for his dealing with the world. Thus in this tradition the tension between three and one is resolved by placing the diversity of revelation *in front of* an emphasis on God's oneness in his essential being. There are dangers with this approach as it seems to separate revelation from the divine essence. Karl Barth points out, 'The reality of God in his revelation is not to be bracketed with an 'only', as though somewhere behind his revelation there stood another reality of God, but the reality of God which meets us in revelation is His reality in all the depths of eternity.' (op. cit. p548.) Despite the need to be cautious towards this doctrinal approach, such a Trinitarian method might offer some model for ecclesiology, in suggesting the way in which we might relate a rich diversity to an underlying unity. The rest of the chapter attempts to do this in terms of the limits of perception and the need to use paradox to enable us to handle 'multi-dimensional truth'. Economic Trinitarianism offers a similar perspective from God's side, viz. that the rich diversity of the church can be seen as divine gift, offered so that the God-given diversity in humanity itself may approach God in a variety of ways. What follows from this is the recognition that if underlying this diversity there is the divine unity, then we must not absolutise our diversities but embrace one another because of the oneness of God underlying all reality.

9. Hilary of Poitiers, 'On the Trinity' II.6.

10. 'On the Trinity' II.7.

11. John of Damascus, 'Exposition of the Orthodox Faith'. I.4.

12. 'On the Trinity', II.7.

13. See the hymn inspired by this incident written by George Rawson (1807-1889). The first verse is:

> We limit not the truth of God
>   To our poor reach of mind
> By notions of our day and sect,
>   Crude, partial, and confined;
> No, let a new and better hope
>   Within our hearts be stirred:
> The Lord hath yet more light and truth
>   To break forth from his word.

14. E. Brunner, 'The Word and the World', (London) 1931 pp6-7.

15. John Macquarrie, 'In Search of Deity: An Essay in Dialectical Theism' The Gifford Lectures for 1983-84 (London) 1984 p15.

16. 'In Search of Deity' p174.

17. There are some honourable exceptions to this statement where, at a national level, a number of denominations have united. When this has happened, as in the case of the United Reformed Church in Britain, there will often be written into the basis of union an openness to other denominations and a commitment made to continue the search for a greater unity. Such examples are signs of hope and judgement on the wider church, but their infrequency enables us still to make a sweeping statement about the implicit exclusivity of denominational structures.

THE ECUMENICAL IMPERATIVE

Chapter Seven

VISIBLE VERSUS INVISIBLE

Movements involve *change*. As a result, there will be disagreements about the speed of change and how radical and far-reaching that change should be. There are even people who, wishing to keep things as they are, use the language of a movement in order to disguise the fact that they don't want to move at all. Language becomes important because the key words are often used in different ways to mean different things.

The search for unity is no exception to this. So many people mean so many different things by the word *unity*. If we are serious about *searching* for unity, then we must not pre-judge the detailed *form* a future unity might have. If the presentation of the gospel and the forms of church life are related to the place and culture in which they are expressed, then unity is bound to take different forms in different places. However, in order to search for and work towards the unity of the church, we must attempt to give some meaningful content to the word *unity*.

It is at this point that we have to affirm a basic principle of the ecumenical movement. *Unity is a spiritual concern, yet it must always manifest itself in outward action and change.* Such change should affect the whole of church life: from relationships between individuals to the transformation of organizations, from the healing of personal hurts to the renewal of church structures. This principle is a part of that fundamental, biblical concern that faith should show itself in action and that new life should result in new life styles:

> 'What good is it, my friends, for someone to say he has faith when his actions do nothing to show it? Can that faith save him?' (James 2.14)

There have been those who have argued that unity is a 'spiritual' quality which has little to do with re-organizing the institutional life of the churches. We must face this challenge not only in order to argue against its claims, but so as to define clearly what we do mean by *unity*. This elusive word has often been qualified with the adjective *visible*, which carried with it the idea that any spiritual renewal of the church will have outward and organizational consequences. *Unity* means more than the joining together of organizations and institutions, but it does include the *outward* as well as the *inward* dimensions of church life.[1]

Those who call for *invisible unity* are not so much a clearly defined group as a range of different people, who nonetheless have in common the desire to resist organizational change. They may use the phrase *invisible unity* or they may speak about *real unity* or *spiritual unity* or just plain *unity*. What they share is a suspicion of unity *schemes*, which they believe tackle organizational amalgamations without achieving a renewal of the people who make up the various churches. It is not easy to understand what *real* or *spiritual* unity can mean unless it is manifested in some visible way. However, we need to hear these voices if we are to sharpen our understanding of that future reality towards which the word *unity* might be pointing us.

At first glance a claim for invisible or spiritual unity might seem perfectly proper. The worship of God and the whole concern with spiritual matters recognizes an invisible world which is not easily tied down and examined. 'God is spirit and those who worship him must worship in spirit and in truth'. (John 4.24). When Christians gather for worship, there is a recognition that they worship God not only as part of a church which stretches around the globe, but with an invisible cloud of witnesses which recedes into the past and reaches into the future. If the church can, in part at least, be invisible, then surely it is right to speak of the unity of the church as invisible.

But it isn't as easy as that. We may talk about *the communion of saints*, but it is misleading to confuse that invisible and eternal reality with what is normally meant by *the church*. When we use the words *the church* it is usually with reference to the historical, this-wordly reality which began in Jerusalem, was persecuted by tyrants, adapted to different cultures and which split into many parts and fragments. In terms of church unity we can only talk in any meaningful way of this historical and institutional church. It began with the apostles, has variously been made up of inspired but frail human beings, and today has more variety than can be easily counted.

Talk of invisible unity makes more sense when used as a *critique* of ecumenical efforts rather than as a position in its own right. There are a number of familiar statements, heard in quite different parts of the church, which we may understand as versions of the invisible unity theory.

First, there are those Christians who express frustration at the number of committees which the ecumenical movement seems to throw up. They mutter about the burgeoning bureaucracy and the wasting of time which comes by duplicating the committees and meetings which already happen in the different denominations.

A variation of this attitude is the claim that the church ought to be more concerned about things that matter, such as mission, rather than expending so much time and energy on internal concerns. Christ sent the disciples out to preach the gospel, rather than form committees which try to cobble together pieces of ecclesiastical machinery. The call is seen as a prophetic one to the church. The challenge is the challenge of gaining a correct perspective. How can people put the minutiae of church organization before the crying needs of a lost world?

Secondly, there is the claim of some Christians that 'We already have a spiritual unity, why is there any need for more than this?' This view is often expressed by those who are not happy about a great deal of church organization and who would want to understand the links between Christians as primarily links of *fellowship*. They rightly claim that fellowship is something that Christians can enjoy across denominational boundaries, but they then go on to claim that those denominational boundaries are unimportant. The plea is made, 'It's more important that we love one another than we get involved in the long, difficult and frustrating project of joining our church structures'. That may be so, but *if* we love one another, then certain actions should follow. Those actions should include attempting to deal with the historical and organizational circumstances which distort our fellowship and which stunt the fruit of our love. When we talk about being united in fellowship with other Christians, we are often talking about a selective fellowship which may cross denominational boundaries, yet turn its back on fellow Christians within the same denomination who have a different theological perspective. At the same time, we must acknowledge that just because, for example, some Charismatic Baptists and some Charismatic Catholics are close to each other and sometimes worship together, it does not follow that the Baptist community is reconciled to the Church of Rome.

So the invisible unity argument takes two main forms. On the one hand, it is a plea for spiritual realities rather than organizational ones and spiritual fellowship rather than institutional mergers. On the other hand, there is some concern for priorities, with mission being seen as far more important than the slow task of adapting and servicing ecclesiastical machines. Just as the apostles were to travel light when Jesus sent them out to announce the Kingdom of God, so the church should travel light in its missionary venture.

It must be admitted that there is much truth in these views. Love is paramount, mission *is* the prime task of the church. However, the setting of love *or* organization, mission *or* church structure as alternatives rather than parts of a whole, provides us with a distorted view of the church. We cannot accept these arguments because they do not take the church, creation or the kingdom of God seriously enough.

Taking the Church Seriously

Before we can agree a working definition of unity, we need to reach some agreement in our understanding of the church. This is no easy task, but we can at least begin by attempting to dismiss some of the more common misunderstandings.

In common speech, 'to go to church' means attending a building, and 'to enter the church' often means presenting oneself for ordination. But despite this popular usage, we can affirm that the church is made up of *people*. It is not a building and it is not a caste of professional clergy. The distinction is all too often made between *clergy* and *lay people*, as though they were experts and beginners. Similarly, 'lay person' is a term often used in everyday language to describe an amateur or non-expert and this in fact had its origins in the previous church use of referring to those who were not ordained priests. However, the word *laity* comes from the Greek *laos* meaing *people* and reminds us that one of the main pictures for the church in the New Testament is *the people of God*. All the members of the church – including bishops, priests and others – are laity in the sense that they are all part of the 'people of God'. Ministries within the church are given to build up the people of God and enable them to fulfil their calling as the church.

Another misuse of the word *church* equates it with *denomination*. We speak of the 'various churches' as though each ecclesial unit was a valid and complete expression of the Church of God. Paul's question to the Corinthians, 'Surely Christ has not been divided among you?' (1 Corinthians 1.13) challenges us to face an equally blunt question for today. Do the different denominations offer a legitimate set of choices which enable people to choose between different styles of worship and emphases of theology, or are they an example of the splits which Paul condemned in his letters?

It has been suggested that our regarding the different denominations as alternative choices for the prospective church-goer is a prime example of our modern captivity to the world of consumerism. To see the denominations as choices is to see our relationship to the church as a matter of choosing the kind of product we want to buy, or the kind of leisure activity we want to pursue. It subjectivizes our belonging to the church to the point where we put our interests and wishes above any claims that the church might make on us. To 'take it or leave it' is not the best foundation for belonging to a community. We need to take the church more seriously than that.

The most frequent use of *church*[2] in the New Testament is when the word denotes a local congregation: *the church in Corinth* or *the church in Jerusalem*. This has been the primary sense of the word in the congregationalist traditions, though it must be said that the local congregation should not refer to one group meeting on one side of a street and another group meeting on the other. If we only use the word *church* in this sense, then we are back to consumer subjectivism for there are no claims bigger than my relationship to the local group. We could have a real debate about the question 'How local is the local church?', for while some would identify the local unit as a single congregation, others would think of a town-wide circuit and others a diocese or province. In each case the answer seems to be linked to where the decisions are made. This is because the concept of church must include the seeking of God's will and the responsible discipleship of the community as a group as well as individuals.

But there is a wider use of the word *church* in the New Testament. On occasion, it refers to that cosmic and invisible reality which we sometimes call *the communion of saints*.[3] The stress here is a universal one, proclaiming a comprehensiveness which includes not only all Christians alive today, but also those who have gone before us and those still to come.

To take the church seriously does not mean that we do so at the cost of mission. We shall look at mission more closely when we examine the relationship of the church to the Kingdom of God, but we need to affirm here that the church's prime calling is to worship and mission. These two perspectives reflect the church in relation to God and in relation to the world, but we can also see that *worship* is not an escape from the world and that *mission* is participation in the life and work of God.

Mission, of course, is usually seen as having a number of facets. It refers to the sharing of the gospel in verbal ways that we often call *evangelism*. It also involves the ministry of *service*, healing, reconciliation, social and community action and the struggle for justice. Some Christians will tend to emphasize one part of this mission rather than another. But whichever expression of mission we are dealing with, we have to acknowledge what when Christians seek to engage in mission together, there is need for organization, planning and the offering and using of material resources. Whether it is an evangelistic rally in a football stadium or a warden scheme for the care of elderly people, door to door visitation or a political struggle for human dignity and justice, *mission means people working together, and that involves structure and organization.*

There are those who invite us to see an alternative vision of the church. They remind us that the church began without purpose-built buildings, that an important image for the church is that of the pilgrim of God, travelling light. This radical voice comes to us from different places. It comes from the base Christian communities to be found in many parts of the world, but especially in Latin America. It comes from the radical Christian groups which meet in homes for the breaking of bread and the nourishing of the struggle against injustice, and it comes from the growing number of house churches that are a part of the Charismatic Movement. There seems to be a difference between those informal groups which are made up of people who are also members of more traditional churches and those informal groups which are the sole expression of the church for the group members. In the case of the former type, it seems that there is often a temporary nature to the group: no bad thing when continuity is provided by other means. In the case of the house churches, which are instead of, rather than as well as, the mainstream churches, it is pointed out that they often become very authoritarian. While they may not have highly developed structures, their very simplicity of organization often leads them towards reliance upon dominating forms of personal leadership.

We need to remember that most Christians find themselves in membership of one of the mainstream churches, with all the organizational implications that flow from a large institution which may be centuries old. We return to the challenge that, if we are going to make a difference for most people, we have to talk about a unity which either *ignores* the institutional facts of life or tries to *change* them.

We must not underestimate the frustration which many people feel about the institutional face of the various churches. To adapt a phrase of Paul, 'We are no better than pots of earthenware to contain this treasure' (2 Corinthians 4.7 NEB). But however much we might like something more appropriate than earthenware, it is still better for carrying water than our bare hands. If we reckon that the church has a task to do which involves people working together, then we must accept that social organization is a necessary part of that project. If we believe in the Lordship of Christ, then we must work out what that means for people acting *together* as an organization and not only as individual disciples. If we believe that the Spirit of God is at work transforming this groaning world into a new creation, then we must not shield the world of the church from the transforming power of his Spirit.

Our reflections on the will of God for his church lead us on to reflect upon the redemption of the world. That must be more than the arithmetic addition of individual believers — it must lead us to the redemption of communities, the saving of the social and the taking seriously of the world for which Christ died.

Taking Creation Seriously

Sunday by Sunday countless Christians stand and, as an act of worship and an expression of faith, recite the words of the creed:

> 'We believe in one God,
> the Father, the almighty,
> maker of heaven and earth,
> of all that is,
> seen and unseen.'[4]

We could see this reciting of doctrinal clauses as a listing of beliefs — pieces of information pigeon-holed for posterity. 'We believe *that* God made heaven and earth', a theory to stand alongside other views about the origins of the universe. However, *we should see this recitation of faith as a statement of fundamental attitudes.* The world is not an infinite jumble of component parts, or a chaos of chance collisions, but a universe which finds its origin, its meaning and its destiny in the God who has summoned it out of nothing. This becomes a way of life: faith ceases to be a catalogue of doctrines and becomes a policy statement of how and why to live. A number of implications follow from such a belief.

First, faith in a *Creator* implies a belief that the material world is important and part of God's concern. A number of religions have ignored the material world as being of little importance, or have even gone further and claimed that matter is intrinsically evil. Such attitudes have from time to time affected the Christian church. A number of traditional, so-called 'Christian' values can be traced from such an influence and need to be challenged by reflection on the doctrine of creation. For example, the early church was influenced by certain aspects of the hellenistic culture which permeated the ancient western world. This sometimes led to the assumption that the human body was somehow evil and so spiritual giants tried to subdue the body by horse-hair vests and flagellation. A further implication was the belief that any kind of sexual activity was evil and to be avoided.

But the belief in God as creator implies that the material world has a divine origin and a divine sustainer. The material world is to be valued for its own sake and because it is a gift of God. In the Bible there is a recurring emphasis on the theme of *stewardship*. In Genesis humankind is shown to us as the steward of creation. A parable of Jesus describes the Kingdom of God in terms of those who are entrusted with cash which is to be used and invested. This theme has an obvious relevance for the church. The church is a human institution, using finite resources in the service of God and humanity. A concern for the institution is not an example of being shackled to earth, but a participation in God's on-going creation. A concern for resources and their deployment is not money-grubbing and base wheeling and dealing, but responsible stewardship of the gifts of God. Belief in creation involves a recognition that the world is part of God's will and that our living and planning and acting in the world are also part of his will. If he had wanted us to keep our heads in the clouds he wouldn't have planted our feet on the earth!

But, secondly, as well as being concerned about the origin and present status of the material world, we are also concerned about its eternal destiny. Paul's vision was of the whole creation groaning in anticipation of the transforming redemption which is part of God's plan (Romans 8.19-22). We sometimes miss the point of John 3.16. We are so concerned about the goodies on offer in the form of eternal life that we miss the mainspring of God's salvation – 'For God so loved the *world* that he gave his only son . . .'

A belief in creation leads us from the past and the present into God's future. It implies a hope of redemption not just for the souls of the righteous (whatever that means) but for the whole of the created material universe. Belief in the resurrection of the body is a part of that fundamental attitude to the world where we see the stuff of the universe not as a launchpad to heaven, but as part of the raw materials which ultimately will be transformed into a new creation. A belief in creation as such will only take us so far. It will mean we stay in Genesis with the glory of the world and, eventually, the patience of God in the covenant to Noah. However, the dynamic of the gospel moves us from *creation* to *redemption*: from a world made new and spoilt by sin to a world made good, as a craftsman would put it. But none of this leaves the world behind. The cross was planted firmly in the earth, even if it pointed to the sky. Jesus took bread and wine and in those everyday things he promised the redemption of the every day. For the church this means that there is even hope for committees, as there is no limit to the redemptive power of God!

Thirdly, this redemption of the world is a reminder that the old categories of sacred and secular, material and spiritual, begin to lose their grip on reality. Just as we should not try to think of a person as an entity made up of two separate parts, of body and spirit, so we should not try to separate the spiritual reality of the church from its actual, phyisical reality. Belief in creation implies the belief that our existence in a world of time and space is the will of God. *Salvation doesn't happen in some rarified world of the spirit, but is God's action in this material world.* To talk of 'spiritual unity' as though it could not be expressed in the actual happenings of this world, is to turn our backs on God and to go in search of an imaginary world, where we construct the rules because it is composed of our own fantasies.

If *this* world is the work of God, then it is his will that his purposes be acted out in this world. Those religious traditions which have emphasised the gulf between the material and the spiritual have tended to be traditions which have stressed the use of theological speculation rather than the humble response to God's self-revelation. This is only to be expected, because revelation is about God disclosing himself in the material world, not a coy deity enticing us to attempt flights of speculative, but oh so spiritual, fantasies.

If we move from belief in a God who has created the world to the belief that the same God has become embodied in a human life, we can see how much of the Christian belief about the world pushes us to affirm the unity of the material world and the purposes of God.

If we talk about life in this world of time and space as *history*, then we can see how God has worked *through* this history. We are created as historical beings. Through Abraham and his descendants God has called people to a historical response. The laws of Moses were a transforming of the Hebrews from a rabble of runaway slaves into an ordered community which tried to reflect the justice of God in its national life. It is through the *history* of this nation, its life in the world of space and time, that God revealed himself and prepared the world for his revelation in Christ.

In Jesus Christ, God worked through history in a unique way. Once and for all we must put aside distinctions between spiritual and physical, because the Word has become flesh. Once and for all we must put aside any belief that the material world is not part of God's plan or not destined to be transformed by his love, for the Word has become flesh. Once and for all we must put aside any misconception about how the physical world is not very important, because the Word has become flesh.

With the Incarnation we can see that God is concerned for the material world. He doesn't fight evil with the pen, or with a battle of ideas. The word becomes *flesh*, a part of the world that is to be transformed, a part of the material creation that some had written off as evil or unimportant. The Incarnation is God's *Yes* to the world in which we live; as big a *Yes* as the pronouncement that creation was good and as big a *Yes* as the rainbow promise to Noah.

The nature of existence in this world is that it is limited by time and space. We must affirm not only that the Word became flesh, but that it became particular flesh: the Word became First Century, Jewish flesh. That particular flesh was nailed to a cross during the rule of a particular Roman emperor and with the agreement of a particular Roman governor. Similarly, the church is called to be faithful to the call of God in *this* world in which Christ died, not some utopia of our imagination.

This radical recognition of the material purposes of God leaves us no choice. If God has created the flesh, if God has come and lived and died and been raised in the flesh, then *he calls his church to follow – in the flesh*. Visions are all very well, but they must still become flesh as the Word became flesh. Indeed, it is the contradiction between vision and reality that provides the setting for crucifixion and, ultimately, resurrection. When Jesus called on people to follow him, it was in this historical sense of embodying the vision in the real world. His promise of a cross testifies to this and reminds the church that words which do not become flesh are not the words of faithful disciples.

Before the end of the first century, the church encountered a tendency to undervalue the physical reality of Jesus. Hellenistic influences led some to say that the Word only *seemed* to be flesh, that the physical body of Jesus was rather like the mask that Greek actors used to wear for a stage performance. The name for this heresy, for that is what it was branded, was *Docetism*. This name came from the Greek *DOKEIN (to seem)* and suggested that Jesus merely appeared to be human.[5]

As early as the first letter of John this view was being attacked. There we find a concern both for the accessibility of God's revelation (I John 1.1-2) and the belief that Christ's coming in the flesh has ethical implications for his followers. The author seems to be tackling that view which says that because the spiritual world and the physical world are separate it doesn't matter what we do in this world. This gnostic view resulted in all kinds of immoral practices. But, logically, this position isn't very far from that view which today says that spiritual unity is all that is required – it doesn't matter how we treat each other in the historical life of the churches. This comparison might seem extreme, but we must respond to the call of God in the word made flesh by faithfulness in the flesh.

All this might seem a long way from the ecumenical debate, but it is not. That Christ came in the flesh provides the basis for the existence of the church, and indeed sets the agenda for the way in which the church is to live. At the centre of the church's worship there is Word and Sacrament. The word is the prophetic preaching which enables the congregation to embody in its own life the call of the gospel. Authentic preaching leads to the life of the church in the world, rather than a speculative titillation which encourages the all-too-human attempts to escape the world. The sacraments use water, bread and wine to embody the faith of the church and the activity of God. These earthy things remind the church that it is called to live in history, within the limitations of time and space, commonly called *the real world*. It is a small leap from the breaking of bread to the political struggle for dignity and justice. It is an even shorter jump from the sharing of a loaf to the belief that the church should be united in as real a way as the ripping of a crust and the chewing of bread.[6]

God's redemption of the church is only *spiritual* in so far as it is *real* and *actual*. But then, this is nothing new. God has acted in the world and called people to live as disciples in the world. The followers of Christ are expected to exercise faith because they are in *this* world, not the next.

Taking the Kingdom Seriously

At the beginning of his Gospel, Mark tells his readers that after the baptism and temptation of Jesus and after the arrest of John the Baptist:

> *'Jesus came into Galilee proclaiming the gospel of God: 'The time has arrived; the kingdom of God is upon you. Repent, and believe the gospel.''* (Mark 1.14b-15)

The kingdom of God is at the heart of the mission of Jesus and is a theme which weaves its way through the Bible. It is, of course, a picture drawn from human experience.

The theme of God as king over Israel, and even over the whole world, is one which runs through the Old Testament.[7] Like other pictures drawn from human experience in order to describe God, the picture of God as king interacts with the expectations people had about the way an earthly king should or did behave. In expecting the king to be the protector of the people and the upholder of justice, the Old Testament sees this as a role given by God in the anointing of the king and a role which reflects God's own kingship. Protection of the nation and the defence of the poor and oppressed is claimed by the prophets to be a charge placed on the king and the rulers quite simply because it is God's will and God's work. This picture of a compassionate monarch is widened when we remember that the image of king is not the only one which is applied to God and that placing other images alongside it enriches both our understanding of God's kingship and our expectations of human kingship. For example, the theme of God as shepherd does not conflict with the picture of God as king, but deepens our comprehension of divine sovereignty and informs our job description for a human ruler.[8]

In the New Testament the emphasis is not so much on God as king, as on his kingdom, those places where his sovereignty is acknowledged. This sovereignty has two sides to it. On the one hand there is the announcing that God *is* king and on the other hand there is the kingship. This is very close to the Hebrew concept of *covenant*, where a covenant was an agreement between two parties – often a lord, or king, and his subjects. Thus the central theme of covenant in the Old Testament is in part about God's *election* of Israel and Israel's *response* in the following of the Law. Laws provided a framework for the kingdom of God in that they were intended to create a community founded on justice and peace. So Jesus announces that the kingdom of God is near, or at hand, or amongst his listeners, and also seeks to elicit from them a response which in turn becomes part of God's rule.

As well as the tension between these two aspects of the kingdom, which we might call the *vertical* tension between God's kingship and the human response, there is what we could call a *horizontal* tension between the present and the future. Not only is it announced that the kingdom is here, it is also promised that the kingdom will come. These are different aspects of a basic human dilemma: 'If God is king, why is the world the way it is?' It was a question asked in the Old Testament and one still asked today. The New Testament responds indirectly by providing a picture of the kingdom which has this two-dimensional tension. On the one hand there is a tension between God being king and the covenant response of his subjects and, on the other hand, there is the tension, or mystery, of the kingdom which is *here*, but which is still to come in its fullness. Yet even this paradox is not sufficient, for we can argue from the New Testament that the kingdom has already come in its fullness in Jesus Christ.

But if we argue this way then we must go on to show that God is not *fully* defined by being called *king*. Rather, the nature of his kingdom is demonstrated by the life, teaching, death and resurrection of Jesus Christ. The one who embodies the kingdom rides a donkey and washes feet. The one who embodies the kingdom spends time in bad company and fights the dehumanizing forces of disease, hypocrisy and selfishness. The ministry of Jesus demonstrates the kingdom. It *is* the kingdom. We could say that in Jesus the kingdom is present in its fullness in one place. Elsewhere and afterwards the kingdom is partly present in more places. The New Testament writings go on to talk about Christ being involved in the final, full manifestation of the kingdom, so that we can be assured that the final kingdom will have the same identity as that which we see in Jesus. It could be argued that the resurrection was the first manifestation of this coming kingdom, in so far as it underlines in power the kingdom which humanity had crucified. The *No* of Good Friday was contradicted by the *Yes* of Easter Day.

The New Testament goes on to see the activity of the Spirit of God in the church as a foretaste of that which is to come. What is also clear is that claims concerning the work of the Spirit always need to be tested by their fruit. In other words, those things which people do or plan or want in the name of the Spirit of God are tested against what we have seen of the kingdom in Jesus.

The community which the Spirit creates is even called *the Body of Christ*, for the kingdom displayed in Jesus is the kingdom which the church is called to serve and embody. This is an important statement, because we must never fall into the trap of equating the church with the kingdom. *Jesus is Lord* became one of the earliest confessions of faith, but it is not to be seen as a magic formula or a party slogan. It only has meaning in so far as it is *lived*. To return to the tensions of the kingdom, the statement about the Lordship of Jesus is not only a statement about his status in an abstract, or even cosmic, sense, but is also an acknowledgement of his sovereign demands on the life of those who are now his subjects.

The church thus becomes part of the kingdom in so far as Jesus is allowed to be Lord of the church. The phrase 'allowed to be' ought not to be shocking, for Jesus comes as the crucified one, at the mercy of those who owe him their allegiance.

The relationship of the church to the kingdom should be an intimate one, but it has to be said that the church as an institution, and individuals who call themselves Christians, can stand outside the kingdom. A more helpful picture may be that of the church within, but only part of, the kingdom.

How will we ever know? The Spirit is tested in the New Testament by comparing the activities in question with what we know of Jesus. The classic description of his mission in terms of the kingdom of God is given us by Luke, who tells of Jesus returning to his home village of Nazareth and explaining the significance of his coming in the words of the book of Isaiah:

'The spirit of the Lord is upon me because he has anointed me;
he has sent me to announce good news to the poor,
to proclaim release for prisoners and recovery of sight for the blind;
to let the broken victims go free,
to proclaim the year of the Lord's favour.' (Luke 4.18f)

Here is present and future. Here is a description of what the coming of the kingdom means and thus a description of the ministry of Jesus. It is also an agenda and a hope − a vision to motivate action, which thrusts us towards the bringing together of God's hope for the world, and the world itself. Many of the Old Testament laws were intended to create this kind of situation within the community. The prophets did not work in a vacuum, for they accused Israel of neglecting the path that had already been made clear. So the kingdom anticipated by the prophets and made clear in Jesus becomes the mission of a church which is made up of the followers of Jesus. Their Lord is the one whose lordship is expressed in these terms of good news to the poor, release for the captive and hope for the despairing.

Servant of the Kingdom

How does the church relate to the kingdom? God is not limited to the church and signs of the kingdom can be identified outside the church, so what is the nature of the relationship between church and kingdom?

First, the church is called to be a *servant* of the kingdom. Ultimately, it is not the church which matters, but the kingdom. What is important is that creation reaches its intended goal of being filled with the glory of God – relationships of love and justice, a living in harmony, *shalom*. The church engages in mission – whether it be evangelism, caring or the struggle for justice – not for the sake of its own survival or prestige, but for the sake of the kingdom of God.

So the church serves the kingdom, in the sense that the picture of the kingdom of God points us to that reality that we have glimpsed in Christ. To follow this man Jesus is to seek to announce and demonstrate the kingdom he embodied. To call him *Lord* is to recognize that the kingdom in him is the centre of all reality, the imperative of all action and the aim of all living.

Part of the kingdom can be seen as those harmonious relationships which are found when people are reconciled. The Gospel is described as the good news of reconciliation and this reconciliation takes place in both the areas of tension that we mentioned above. The tension between the God who is King and his subjects who reject him, and the tension between the world as it is and the world as it shall be. Paul describes the gospel as 'the saving power of God' – the means whereby the kingdom is implemented. So the church serves the kingdom by *announcing* the Gospel – the good news that the kingdom has come in Christ. But the church continues to serve by *demonstrating* the arrival of the kingdom in its own life and by inviting others to share in this revolutionary reality. This suggests a closer relationship than simply one of service, and we are forced to go on and use other pictures for the relationship between church and kingdom.

Sign of the Kingdom

So, secondly, the church is called to be a *sign* of the kingdom, something which points towards the reality. This must be more than simply preaching or announcing. Here we are acting out the kingdom, a non-verbal demonstration of the reality towards which the world is being led.

The idea of the *sign* is a very important one in the Bible. Israel is called to be a sign for the nations. When the nations look at the chosen people, their eyes are not intended to stay on the national equivalent of teacher's pet –

the reality of Israel's community life was intended to point beyond itself to the God who was its King. It seems that Jesus was often asked for signs to prove to the sceptical that he was sent from God. While he rejected such appeals, there is a sense in which his whole ministry was full of signs. These actions were not to be seen as someone showing off with arbitrary acts of power, but the actions themselves were a part of the kingdom towards which they are pointing. This is important because we must define a sign as not merely a pointer, but something which *participates* in the reality to which it is pointing. So when John the Baptist, puzzled in prison, sent his disciples to Jesus to ask:

> ''Are you the one who is to come, or are we to expect someone else?' Jesus answered, 'Go and report to John what you hear and see: the blind recover their sight, the lame walk, lepers are made clean, the deaf hear, the dead are raised to life, the poor are brought good news – and blessed are those who do not find me an obstacle to faith.'' (Matthew 11.3b-6)

Now if the church is to be a sign of the kingdom and a pointer which participates in the reality itself, then it is not enough to talk about the church *preaching* the kingdom. The demands of the calling of the church are that the reality which is *preached* be also the reality which is *lived* by the church. Just as this is true for individual disciples, so this is true for the institution. To preach a gospel of reconciliation, to be a sign of the shalom community, means living the kingdom, living and practising reconciliation.

The ecumenical implications of this ought to be fairly clear. It is not enough to talk about *invisible unity* when the church is called to be a *sign* of the kingdom. The problem with invisible unity is that it cannot be seen. What *are* seen are the inherited divisions fed by wasteful isolation and fearful competition. Talk of invisible unity will only maintain this situation where the credibility of a reconciling gospel is brought into question.

But how can this human organization, this bunch of repentant sinners, embody the kingdom of God? We need to put the question even more strikingly, for the relationship of church to kingdom is closer still.

Foretaste of the Kingdom

The church is called to be a *foretaste* of the kingdom of God. The church is able to be a sign, not only because it must try to copy the example of Christ, not only because it must try to demonstrate the kind of world God wants, but *because God has given his Spirit.*

The claim of the story of Pentecost is that God is working powerfully in the lives of those who respond to Jesus. The divisions of humanity portrayed in the story of the Tower of Babel (Genesis 11) are reversed as boundaries of language, and therefore culture, are transcended. This Spirit is God himself – the God who was, and is, active in creation; the God who worked in the ministry of

Jesus and the God who continues to work by transforming the lives of men and women. Paul describes the reality of God working in people's lives as a foretaste, a down-payment or guarantee, of what is to come (II Corinthians 1.22 and Ephesians 1.14).[9]

So the church is to be a foretaste of the future kingdom by being an expression of the present kingdom. The reality of the church's life is not merely a human attempt at right living, *external* from God, but a *participation* in the whole providential activity of the Spirit which is poured out at Pentecost and is working in the transformation of the created world:

> '. . . the universe itself is to be freed from the shackles of mortality and is to enter upon the glorious liberty of the children of God . . . We also, to whom the Spirit is given as the firstfruits of the harvest to come, are groaning inwardly while we look forward eagerly to our adoption, our liberation from mortality.'
> (Romans 8, part of verses 21 and 23)

If we believe that God is at work through his Spirit, transforming and re-creating the church, then we must expect the church to show the new creation in its life. If visible unity means taking *creation* seriously, then we also have to say that it means taking *salvation* seriously, by being a foretaste of the kingdom.

Just as the church is called to be a sign and a foretaste, so it has within it certain signs which help it to realize its calling. For example, the fellowship of the eucharist is a sign of that peace which God wills for the whole of creation, but is also demands of those who come to the table that they be at peace with one another. In being reconciled to each other they become a foretaste of that future kingdom which they pray for when they cry *Marana tha*, 'Come, Lord Jesus, come'.

Connections

It is, of course, artificial to deal with the church, creation and kingdom as separate realities. To take the church seriously, we need to recognize its place within the purposes of God as a sign of the transformed creation and the coming kingdom. We must not talk of the kingdom as though it were a different world from the world in which we live – the new creation is a transformation of the old, a resurrection not a replacement. The kingdom of God is God's rule in the kingdoms of this world, a challenging of the powers and structures which enslave people here and now. It was the kingdom of Rome which crucified the King of the Jews, it was the powers of organized religion and vested interest which refused to recognize in the coming of the man from Nazareth the coming of the kingdom of God.

It does not make sense to be satisfied with the structural divisions of the church unless it can be argued that those divisions are the will of God. To claim that God wants reconciliation, and yet to be happy with structures which push people apart and perpetuate misunderstanding and division, is to drive a wedge between God and the world that Christ came to save. Just as Jesus called men and women to follow as practical disciples, so he calls the church to practical discipleship.

We must now turn to the relationship of ecumenism to mission. But we shall continue to encounter the inter-relatedness of all that we explore. For mission is to do with the kingdom, misson takes place in the world and mission is the calling of the church. Ecumenical activity is not simply good stewardship when it comes to mission, it is also good mission.

Notes

1. Another word which carries a similar idea is *organic* unity. Central to the argument of this chapter is the link between the inward (or spiritual) and the outward (or physical, historical, organization). In so far as *organic* is a biological word it can qualify *unity* by suggesting the inter-relatedness of all aspects of the church's life. However, *visible* has been used in the text of this chapter because of its use in Twentieth Century ecumenical affirmation and documents.

2. The Greek word *EKKLESIA* is probably best translated *assembly*. In the Pauline epistles the reference is to the church/assembly in a particular place and clearly focusses our attention on the people.

3. Eg. Colossians 1.18 and Ephesians 5.23-27.

4. This is the beginning of the Nicene-Constantinopolitan Creed, but see also the Apostles' Creed which begins:

> '*I believe in God, the Father almighty,*
> *creator of heaven and earth*'.

5. See chapter II note 19.

6. The shocking language of John 6.51 and 54, where believers are said to crunch the flesh of Jesus and drink his blood, is probably a bold attempt to counter docetic tendencies amongst the first readers and, according to Dunn, is even in the written 'Signs Source' used by the evangelist. See 'Unity and Diversity' pp300-304.

7. The psalms are particularly eloquent in their announcing of the kingship of God. Psalm 2 may well have been a coronation psalm and both emphasises his lordship over the kings of the earth (v2) and announces that the king of Israel is God's adopted son (v7). Here the link between God's power and the power of the king is most closely expressed, but the converse is also true: as God's son, the king must reign in a way appropriate to God's son. This earthly rule of the king must bear the character of God's rule. Certainly, the kings were often targets of the prophetic denunciation when they were not

judged to be living up to their calling and failing to apply God's laws to their method of government or leadership of the nation.

8. The traditions about David are particularly strong in linking the themes of king and shepherd. See especially the stories of David's origins and the words of the northern tribes' invitation when they requested him to be their king: 'To you the Lord said, 'You are to be shepherd of my people Israel; you are to be their prince'' (2 Samuel 5.2). Of particular interest when linking the themes of king and shepherd are the words of Ezekiel 37.24: 'My servant David will be king over them; they will all have one shepherd. They will conform to my laws and my statutes and observe them faithfully.'

There is an interesting link between the image of God as king and God as shepherd in those Orthodox churches where the Shepherd icon has replaced the Pantecrator (God as king and judge).

9. The Greek *ARRABON* is a commercial word meaning, pledge or deposit. The suggestion is of a part payment of that which is later to be paid in full. Thus the initial payment is a guarantee that the promise to pay in full will be honoured, but it is also part of that final payment. The Spirit is therefore both a pledge of full salvation in the future and the activity of the same God who will complete his purposes for creation. The church can therefore be seen as the promise of God and a part of his future purpose. Examples of reconciliation and unity both encourage us that there is more to come, by God's grace. But they are also a part of that future, graciously brought into the present time.

Chapter Eight

INSIDE OUT

Virtue or Necessity?

Let me take you to Swindon, half-way between London and South Wales. In the early seventies, the local council of churches challenged all the congregations in the centre of the town to come together in order to form one united, worshipping congregation. Five of the congregations in the centre of that expanding town accepted the challenge and, over a period of six years, worked more closely together until they were one congregation under one roof.

One of the redundant buildings, belonging to a congregation of the Churches of Christ, was sold and was then used as a community centre. Another building, the Methodist Central Hall, was sold and most of the proceeds used to build a new, ecumenical church on a new estate at the edge of the town. With some of the remaining money the Methodists purchased a share in one of the other church sites – the Baptist land, where now a new, purpose-built ecumenical centre has been built. The local Baptist church invested that Methodist money and used the income to pay for a minister who served the new community which had begun to worship in the new ecumenical church on the edge of the town . . .

And so the story could continue. A United Reformed Church site, (formerly Congregationalist), was re-developed and income was used to provide a manse and part of a church extension in other areas of population expansion in the town. Meanwhile, another URC building (formerly Presbyterian) was used by the central united congregation for its worship and service for more than a decade until the new church centre was complete. Agreements, buildings and amalgamations are only part of a story and cannot convey the exciting, dynamic life of the new united congregation which entered a period of considerable service and ecumenical witness in the town centre.

Similar stories can be told from different parts of England where local Ecumenical Projects have made all kinds of sharing possible. This particular story has been told because of the way in which the coming together of these congregations released land and money which could be used in vital church work elsewhere. However, there will inevitably be a number of different reactions to this scheme and others like it.

There will be those who say that it is a fine example of stewardship and that more churches, in an era of dwindling numbers, ought to do the same. But there will be those who will argue that here is another example of the churches losing ground in down-town areas and that these churches were simply reacting to the inevitable rather than responding to the visionary. The argument runs that inevitable social forces had left these once prosperous churches stranded, rather like islands after a flood. They have made an ecumenical virtue out of an economic necessity.

It can be pointed out that these particular churches joined while they were still vigorous, unlike many others who have dwindled beyond the point of no return. Nonetheless, the argument is a common one and is part of that larger view which sees the ecumenical movement as a last ditch stand, a re-allocation of dwindling resources before the onslaught of secularization. It is argued that the tide of faith has gone out and that ecumenism is attempting to cut a few channels for water that is already seeping away.

Allied to this view is the judgement of some sociologists[1] that ecumenism is primarily a movement led by professional clergy who are trying to shore up the institutions that give them status in a situation where this institutional base is being eroded. However, we should note that this criticism was largely voiced in the 1960's and that in recent years in Britain the clergy have often been identified as more of a hindrance than a help in the cause of unity.[2] It is also suggested that the churches are acting rather like businesses in a market economy. The creation of a cartel[3] enables the creation of a stronger unit in an environment, whether ecclesiastical or economic, that favours size and where viability is linked to market-share.

There are two points which need to be made. First, we need to take account of the churches' own understanding of what they were about before we make final decisions about what we believe was going on in the way of social processes. While it is sometimes argued[4] that ecumenical rhetoric bears little relation to the 'real' reasons for union, this claim misunderstands the way in which vision and reality affect each other. Large-scale social trends may well be identified by a social historian as the main cause of a church union; however, such a view seems to ignore the main participants' view of what is happening. For those churches in Swindon, vision did play a large part in the decision to change, in the resolving of differences and in the convincing of waverers. Such an account has every right to be taken as seriously as the analysis of social trends.

Secondly, it cannot be denied that the self-confessed motives of those who came together were a mixture of the theological and non-theological. But even the non-theological motives need to be understood sympathetically and reflected on *theologically*.

For example, the rationalization of plant, finance and personnel could be seen as a non-theological strategy for union. However, such a strategy can and should be defended on the grounds that a rational use of resources is good stewardship. The theme of stewardship is a biblical one and the belief that God entrusts us with resources which we must use wisely is a view which can be defended theologically as well as economically. In recent years, stewardship campaigns have brought home to many local congregations the need for care in financial planning and sacrifice in financial giving. Such stewardship is not seen as a lack of faith but quite the opposite. Great faith is being exercised when budgets are planned in an *expenditure led* way. Similarly, the wise use of resources can be based on both the doctrine of creation (Genesis 1.28) and the parable of the talents (Matthew 25.14-30).

The doctrine of creation relates to the theme of stewardship by affirming that this world has meaning. The stuff of the universe: land, human society, and the money and buildings which go with it, are all 'significant'. They are *significant* in a double sense – in *themselves* they are things which have been created by God and pronounced 'good' (Genesis 1.1-31), and, as *signs*, they signify their origin, the reality of God the creator. *Stewardship is in part a recognition that creation is to be included within our worship*, for as creatures, the stuff of the universe is the medium within which we have our being and within which we are called to act.

This leads to the theme of the talents. It is probable that the original intention of the parable was a critique of the scribes and Pharisees, who seemed so concerned to keep their religion safe that it became sterile rather than fruitful.[5] However, the framework of the story is of stewards who are entrusted with wealth and expected to use it in such a way that it increases. Just as the early church and the evangelists developed this story with wider applications relevant for new settings, so we can develop its usefulness while keeping within the basic thrust of the original story.

So, in keeping to the theme of stewardship, we can claim that we are entrusted with our lives and all they contain. We are entrusted with our bodies, with places, with occasions, with companions, with money and resources. Not only are we called to use the stuff of creation in our worship but we are called to follow in the world. *Discipleship happens within history, within the concrete limits and possibilites of a particular situation.* We are trapped and enabled by creation as an artist is both limited and set free by the chosen medium of wood, paint or music. Because of human sin we can see that our response is going to be woefully inadequate. Yet we are called to follow: not leaving this world, but witnessing and serving within it. This means that the raw materials for our discipleship, the raw materials for mission, need to be recognized, offered and used. Thus bricks and mortar, personnel and investment income, are all factors which we need to reflect on theologically if they are to be used faithfully.

We also need to ask about other factors in the process of uniting which might be judged as non-theological. For example, the use of money for a new church building in another part of the town can be explained as both an example of missionary concern and an act of selfless sharing in releasing resources for use in that way. While wider church organizations were inevitably involved in the discussions and planning in Swindon, it was not a matter of bureaucratic leaders moving the money around. Rather, there was a concern on the part of local Christians to respond to the needs of the new area as well as wanting to respond to the town centre from a position of united strength, rather than divided weakness. We could discuss the tactics of size in great detail, but here the local decisions reflected the belief that in a town centre situation a substantial congregational base would make possible mission projects which could not be contemplated by smaller groups. Bigger is not necessarily better, but neither is small always beautiful. The important point here is not a universal principle about large or small, but a concern to respond to the missionary needs of a situation in an appropriate way. Thus mission and unity belong together when local Christians respond together to the needs on their doorstep.

This is not to dismiss the sociological interpretation of events in this story or others like it. It is rather a plea to place alongside such a view the self-understanding of the participants as a valid part of what was happening. There is a parallel here with the so-called *paradox of grace*. When we speak of the Holy Spirit working in someone's life we are not denying that there are psychological and other factors at work; but, in the paradox of grace, we hold in tension two different interpretations of what is happening. In a similar way we can speak of God at work in history. Such a claim does not make the historian redundant, but provides another interpretation of reality which is held alongside the critical historical view.

A Question of Credibility

This principle of theological reflection on non-theological factors is an important one. It is a mistake to think that we must always begin with a theological truth which is then applied to a specific situation. Christian action will often be interpreted as response to social forces. Both views need to be held together, enabling a dynamic dialogue between the pressures of a situation and the theological reflection on that situation. Such a relationship between so-called non-theological factors and a theological reflection on them looms large in the ecumenical movement whenever we talk about *credibility*. The argument is often presented that the unity of the church is necessary in order to offer a credible witness. This can mean a number of things.

First, it can justify the amalgamation of several weak units in order to provide what is seen as one viable unit. What is judged as *viable* might relate to the necessary up-keep of a church building or the maintenance of a paid minister. In either case, there will be those critics who point out that both clergy and buildings are part of the institutional baggage of the church and that neither are either desirable or necessary for the continuing witness of the people of God. The house church movement and the base Christian communities are examples of this prophetic voice. [6]

However, if we acknowledge that many people will wish to relate to the church in larger groups, and that forms of community action (from evangelism to schemes of care) need crowds rather than groups, then accommodation, paid leadership and viable numbers become factors which lead to a *steward-ship response* to the situation. This means that credibility is linked with the willingness to marshall sufficient resources to meet the missionary challenge. Credibility is judged by the way in which the mission of the churches over-comes their differences. It has been argued that this was a factor in the formation of the Church of South India in 1947 when an awareness of the missionary needs of the subcontinent overcame the inherited divisions of the various denominations.

Secondly, the claim to credibility can be used to make a quite different point. In John 17.20f Jesus prays:

> 'It is not for these alone that I pray, but for those also who through their words put their faith in me. May they all be one: as you, Father, are in me, and I in you, so also may they be in us, **that the world may believe** that you sent me.'

Here the prayer for unity is based on the assumption that the credibility of the witness of the church is linked to its being united. The love of the Christian believers for each other substantiates the claims of their preaching and provides evidence to support their claim that God was at work in Christ, and that his love is at work in the transformed lives of the Christian community. In John 13.34-35 Jesus gives his disciples a new commandment, but then links their obedience to the credibility of their witness:

> 'I give you a new commandment: love one another; as I have loved you, so you are to love one another. If there is this love among you, then everyone will know that you are my disciples.'

Credibility is again seen to involve a direct link between the content of the preaching and the life of the community doing the preaching. This is very close to our argument in the previous chapter about visible expressions of spiritual unity. There, we saw the doctrines of creation and incarnation making it necessary for the church to provide a social expression of the truths it proclaims. Here, we move from pragmatic arguments and their religious significance to practical arguments where the life of the community is aligned to its message and self-understanding.

We are brought back to the biblical themes which we have already explored. Now their importance is brought from the realm of bible study or theological debate and is placed in the high street and the market place. If the church is called to make incarnate its message then the arguments in favour of ecumenism spring from the very heart of the gospel. Unity and mission are inseparable.

Inside Out

Unity and mission are inseparable because the church doesn't live for itself: it is a community which exists because it has been *called*. This is an assertion about the *purpose* of the church rather than an analysis of its historical origins. Sociologically, we could find many non-theological reasons why churches exist in their present form or why individual people belong to particular churches. The church's own understanding of its function is usually described in terms of *mission*. It is a community with a purpose which it identifies both with the biblical account of the call to Israel as the people of God and Jesus' calling of his disciples. The church begins with the initiative of God, who in Jesus Christ acts to redeem the world. This is gospel, or good news, and this gospel is both the reality which summons the church into existence and the reality which shapes the church for its mission – the proclaiming of that gospel in the world. The writer of the First Letter of Peter describes the purpose of the church in terms reminiscent of the description of Israel's call in Exodus 19.1-6.

> 'But you are a chosen race, a royal priesthood, a dedicated nation, and people claimed by God for his own, to proclaim the glorious deeds of him who has called you out of darkness into his marvellous light.' (1 Peter 2.9)

We cannot separate any *inner* meaning of the church from its *outer* life. There is no inner, mystical reality which exists separately from this call to proclaim the triumphs of God. The inner realities have to be made manifest in the outward life of the community. In turn, this outer life of proclamation and service is the meaning of the inner reality. This is the heart of incarnation: *the gospel determines the church*. This means that the preaching of the gospel summons people to faith and at the same time this very gospel has at its heart the dynamics which push the church outside itself.

Because the gospel is the good news of salvation, the very people who are *saved* are turned inside out. Encounter with Christ brings our selfishness under judgement and creates within us a concern for others. We cannot keep apart the gospel itself and what the gospel achieves in us. Nor can we keep apart its achievement in us and its achieving through us the salvation of others. This is a continuous movement of love from God and in God.

Mission is not an *add-on* to the life of the church – it is at the heart of what the church is called to be. This is both because the church is called to a mission and because the gospel *is* mission. Good news cannot be repressed and God's redeeming love cannot be held up and possessed, for love creates love.

Living Gospel

If we apply this dynamic view of mission to those biblical themes which we explored in chapter 3, we shall see that this provides a fresh basis for ecumenism. If we see that the gospel naturally leads to the church's mission, then we can see how the very nature of the gospel leads to unity. We cannot separate unity from unity-in-mission because the life of the church and its mission are one and the same.

The biblical themes which we studied were peace, reconciliation, unity and love. We can see these as particular ways of expressing the good news of what God had achieved in Christ. Shalom is his will for the world he created and continues to sustain. In Christ he has announced forgiveness and acted for the redemption of the sin which distorts and destroys the world's peace. The church is called to be a community of peace, embodying shalom and living and acting as a sign and foretaste of the shalom God wills for the whole cosmos. The *being* and the *doing* of the church cannot be kept apart – we are all called to be ministers of peace.

The gospel is a gospel of reconciliation. God in Christ reconciles the world to himself and we in turn are reconciled to each other. Thus Paul affirms that those who are reconciled are called to share in the ministry of reconciliation. Here we return to the question of credibility, for it must be asked, 'How can the church preach a gospel of reconciliation unless it seeks reconciliation in its own life?' Mission and unity belong together, for both are caused by God's reconciling action in Christ and both are gathered up to be used by God in the on-going ministry of reconciliation.

Here we can see that the themes of peace and reconciliation belong together. Shalom is the goal of reconciliation, but it is also the means of reconciliation:

> 'Once you were far off, but now in union with Christ Jesus you have been brought near through the shedding of Christ's blood. For he is himself our peace. Gentiles and Jews, he has made the two one, and in his own body of flesh and blood has broken down the barrier of enmity which separated them.' (Ephesians 2.13f)

> 'Spare no effort to make fast with bonds of peace the unity which the Spirit gives.' (Ephesians 4.3)

We could talk of God's *rolling programme of peace and reconciliation*. In Jesus Christ we see the embodiment of God's shalom and the announcing of the Kingdom. Through the cross he is made our peace, reconciling us to God and to each other. We in turn are called to live this peace, to embody this peace, as a sacramental shalom community – to announce this peace and share in the reconciliation that will lead to the widening of God's shalom.

In a similar way we can see how unity and love are linked. The unity for which Paul pleads in his letters is made possible by the exercising of the various gifts in love. Unity is the communal expression of the love which transforms us and which enables us to face ourselves and seek each other.

Love turns us inside out, for what we desired for ourselves we now desire for others. Love turns us inside out, for the love which grasps us is a divine love for the world. We share in its flow by our loving the world as well. This means mission, but it also means unity, for we cannot act in love other than by being drawn together by the bonds of love:

> 'For the love of Christ controls us once we have reached the conclusion that one man died for all and therefore all mankind has died. He died for all so that those who live should cease to live for him who for their sake died and was raised to life . . . For anyone united to Christ there is a new creation; the old order has gone; and a new order has already begun. All this has been the work of God. He has reconciled us to himself through Christ, and has enlisted us in this ministry of reconciliation.' (2 Corinthians 5.14-15,17-18)

Mission and unity belong together because the gospel is a gospel of peace, a gospel of reconciliation, a gospel of love. So the announcing of this gospel must have as its aim the establishing of peace, the achieving of reconciliation, the reaching out and sharing of love. Such aims can only be accomplished by means of peace, by acts of reconciliation and love.

A church which knows of the sacrifices of reconciliation and the extravagance of love is more equipped for the announcing of this gospel than a church which is not. Here is an argument from credibility, but it is more than that. Here is an argument for unity which flows from the heart of the gospel. If the gospel is going to be at the heart of the church, then the church must go in search of unity — for that is to go in search of its real self and to go in search of its real mission.

A Common Calling

Another way in which we can look at the relationship between mission and unity is to see the call of God as a basis for unity. We have already studied how the Faith and Order movement is engaged in a project *Towards the common expression of the apostolic faith today.* The search for such a common expression is the search for an explicit symbol of unity. However, any common expression of the faith which is finally agreed, and indeed the search itself, is over-shadowed by the shared Lordship of Christ.

> 'There is one body and one Spirit, just as there is one hope held out in God's call to you; one Lord, one faith, one baptism; one God and Father of all, who is over all and through all and in all.' (Ephesians 4.4-6)

Here is the claim that the search for unity is inspired by the Spirit of God. The hope which lives in our hearts, and which also stands before us as a vision of God's peace, is an integral part of God's call. We are united by the one God who gives us one hope and enlists us with one call. So a further basis for unity can be found in *the one call of God to his people.* This basis has the advantage that it stands out ahead of us. It is not contradicted by differences in doctrine or disagreements of denominations. The call is grounded in the one God and his purposes for humanity. This call is embodied in the one Lord who calls us to follow. The way in which we follow is constituted by the one who calls. Thus the coming of Jesus Christ is the path which the church is called to walk. The marks of his ministry are to be the marks of the ministry of the church. Here the unity of the church is to be found in the call of Jesus Christ. This is a more profound basis than any theological formulation and it is a more radical basis than any exhortation.

Churches may disagree about the way in which the life of the church is to be ordered. They may disagree about the way in which the gospel is to be expressed. But the call of God is something which is beyond them, not only in the sense that it cannot be grasped, but in the sense that it beckons them forward. Here unity is grounded in God and not in the church, grounded in God's call and in the hope of unity which the call creates.

We can illustrate this by describing the call of God and following through the implications for mission and unity. W.A. Visser 't Hooft did just this in his study *The Pressure of our Common Calling.*[7] He argued that the Church is called to witness, service and fellowship. The three forms of mission correspond to the three classical offices of Christ: the prophetic office corresponds to the call to witness, the priestly office corresponds to the call to fellowship, and the royal office corresponds to the call to service, because in the New Testament lordship is dramatically re-interpreted (eg. Mark 10.45, John 13.12-17, Philippians 2.1-11).

Because unity is inherent in a common call, the churches grow in unity when they respond together to this call. So a common *witness* leads to a recognition of priorities and the agreement in a common gospel. Also, the content of the witnessing is the life of the community in which unity is of the essence. As the church embodies its gospel of reconciliation, so its witnessing leads it to become its true self.

He argued that the call to *service* has both an internal and an external dimension. There is the call to mutual service within the church and there is the call to serve Christ through the world. So the churches are called to serve each other in mutual support and solidarity, thus growing in unity. But they are also called to serve the world, and in fulfilling that service they will grow together.

The churches are called to *fellowship*. We have already seen how in the New Testament KOINONIA means both fellowship and sharing, in both spiritual and material ways. This is ultimately expressed in the sacrament of Holy Communion. This constitutes the fellowship by re-presenting the cross, the central event by which the broken fellowship between God and humanity has been restored. It proclaims the communion between Christ and the believers through it.[8] St. Augustine wrote:

> '*Since then you are the body of Christ and his members, it is your mystery that is placed on the Lord's table; it is your mystery that you receive.*'

and this can be re-phrased:

> '*Since you are the koinonia of Christ, it is your mystery that is placed on the Lord's table, it is your mystery that you receive.*'[9]

The churches are thus called to express their KOINONIA both by the sharing of resources and by the sharing of dialogue. Both these will be more than one-way sharing. Although previous generations will have thought of 'strong' churches in certain countries helping 'weak' churches in other countries, this is not to be so, for we each need to receive from the other. Similarly, *dialogue* must characterize our relationships, where we listen to each other and grow through each other's testimony.

Most important of all, our understanding of KOINONIA needs to inform the mission which is expressed in witness and service. Witness without fellowship between the churches is a contradiction of the gospel of the Lord who died in order to gather into one the scattered children of God. Service which does not participate in the solidarity of fellowship is in danger of becoming mere philanthropy, a condescending service which does not follow the Lord who, though rich, for our sakes became poor.

One Hope Held Out in God's Call

The mission of the church leads us to unity as something which is at the heart of the call of the church. Unity is therefore no optional extra, but a divine imperative which is to be found both within the gospel and in the outworking of the gospel. It is part of the content of mission and the way in which mission is to be undertaken. But unity is also the fruit of mission when it is undertaken in a faithful attempt to live out the gospel.

To recognize the promise of unity in the common calling of God is to locate the promise of full unity in the future. This is a promise of God, but as such it is a future which we must live in the present. This is because the church is called to be an *arrabon*,[10] a foretaste of the shalom which is God's purpose for the whole universe. The church is called to proclaim and live out this hope because unity is not just for the church. Ecumenism is for the whole of creation.

Notes

1. E.g. B. Wilson, 'Religion in Secular Society' (London) 1966.

2. In the 1981 Anglican vote on the proposals for a covenant between five churches in England it was the House of Clergy of the General Synod which failed to provide the necessary two thirds majority. The reports from the Lent 86 discussion groups reflected a widespread view that clergy and hierarchies

126

were responsible for preventing unity and the reason given was 'vested interests'. See 'Views from the Pews' published by the British Council of Churches and the Catholic Truth Society (London) 1986 pp31f and 71f.

3. R. Robertson, 'The Sociological Interpretation of Religion', (Oxford) 1970 pp212; and P.L. Berger, 'The Social Reality of Religion', (London) 1967 pp142.

4. See the chapter 'Ecumenism, the Light that Failed' in J. Kent, 'The Unacceptable Face: The Modern Church in the Eyes of the Historian', (London) 1987 pp203-215.

5. See C.H. Dodd, 'The Parables of the Kingdom', (London) 1935 pp146-153; A.M. Hunter, 'Interpreting the Parables', (London) 1960 pp79-81; J. Jeremias, 'The Parables of Jesus', ET (London) 1963 pp58-63.

6. See L. Boff, 'Ecclesiogenesis' ET (London) 1986; J. Vincent 'The Alternative Church' (Belfast) 1976.

7. W.A. Visser 't Hooft, 'The Pressure of our Common Calling', (London) 1959.

8. Visser 't Hooft pp66-67.

9. Re-phrased in J.G. Davies, 'Members One of Another', (London) 1958 p22.

10. See chapter 7[9].

Chapter Nine

SUMMARY AND SIGNPOSTS

The time has come to look back and to look forward – to survey these reflections and to draw from them indications for the present and directions for the future. The arguments and reflections have attempted to give account of the ecumenical hope. All Christian hope challenges us and beckons us forward along a road which involves repentance, faith and faithfulness. The ecumenical hope is no different, for it offers disturbance and challenge, as well as promise and fulfilment.

There are other books which attempt to discuss different models of unity and the issues involved in union at local and wider levels. There are other places where the reader can find extensive discussion of faith and order issues *within* ecumenism. The present task has been considerably more limited.

Is Unity Important?

In this book, we have attempted to reflect theologically on the question, 'Is the search for the unity of the church important?' The question has been asked from various angles and different theological resources have been used in attempting a response. The result is a *Theology of Ecumenism*. Others must judge its adequacy, but if, in the short term, it helps some to reflect on the theological basis of ecumenism and, in the longer term, encourages others to improve on what is offered here, then it will have done its job.

There may be some who, having read these pages, say that they have seen it all before, that it is 'old hat'. Here is a marshalling of arguments and reflections which attempts to explain why the writer believes the search for unity to be important. For those who are already convinced of this there may be some reflections which enrich or undergird their commitment. For those who are un-convinced, it is hoped that there is something here which may challenge them to look again at their assumptions about the church, its life and its mission.

Because this is a theological reflection rather than a rhetorical exhortation, the phrase *will of God* has been used very sparingly. However, it *is* a term to be found in these pages and an explanation is needed, for we can easily baptize our views with the claim that they are God's will. When the claim has been made in this work that the search for unity is the will of God, it has been at the *end* of an argument. In other words, the theological reflection has taken place first – the probing and exploring of scripture, tradition and the con-temporary situation. The phrase *will of God* has not been used to advance an argument but to acknowledge a conclusion, and this ought to be the way we usually try to discern the divine will.

It could be argued that there is an inevitability about the conclusions reached – they are an accounting for a commitment and, as such, the whole work can be seen as a testimony or an apologetic. The main claim of this book is that the search for unity is neither an optional extra, nor a dangerous diversion. The claim is clear – the search for unity is a search undertaken in response to a divine command. There is an ecumenical imperative which we cannot evade. If the word *command* does not commend itself, then let us use the word *invitation*. We are invited to seek the unity of the church and because of our loving allegiance to the one who invites us, we cannot evade his call.

Theology as a reflective exercise will often lead to abstractions. However, theological reflection can and should lead us back to action. Our explorations in ecclesiology ought to lead us to a questioning of the life of the church. Our vision of hope ought to beckon us on, to live that hope now. Here is theology at work – reflecting on that part of the world we call the church and calling us to live out the implications of our questioning.

The Divine Summons

In our biblical reflections we found themes which reinforced both the importance of unity and the theological basis for approaching it. Reconciling love is what leads us towards God's shalom. This is to be expressed in the church as a foretaste of that which he wills for the whole universe. The peace we exchange at the Eucharist is an expression of this hope, and the bread and wine mediate Jesus, the one in whom that reconciling love has come to us. The search for unity is one which begins with love and moves to love, and it is as though we are caught up into the life of God, for he is one in love and calls us to be one in him.

Ecumenism begins with an encounter and a discovery. It begins when Christians who have experienced the church through only their own denomination meet, listen to and learn from Christians of a different tradition. Whether it is a local study group where Catholics and Baptists discover a common Lord, or a high-level symposium which produces a complex theological statement, ecumenism begins with *encounter*. Theoretical ecumenism has little meaning, because it is speculation born of misunderstanding. It is only when we hear the account of another's faith from that other person that we begin to understand another's faith as something which is alive. It is in the personal encounter that prejudice and ignorance are surprised and persuaded to listen.

We must not romanticize such an encounter, for it is risky and can also lead to continued misunderstanding and retrenched positions. But encounter is a necessary beginning to the ecumenical search. As well as providing data which helps us to understand another Christian perspective, ecumenical meeting also enables us to discover a common bond. We may not be able to express this very clearly, but this existential discovery provides a motivation as well as an object for the beginnings of ecumenical enquiry.

As a result, we need to find a theological framework in which to place this experience. Much of traditional Christian teaching has been passed on through the ethos of one denomination or another. As human beings, we need to belong to a community, and the communities which are available to us are the broken parts of the church. Therefore, the theological framework with which we begin is one constructed of our personal experience, the stories of those who nurtured us in the faith, the worship and practices of our own tradition and the general ethos that carries the name of *Methodist* or *Roman Catholic* or *Pentecostal*.

This needs to be replaced with an *ecumenical* framework – not a disembodied theology, but a theological framework that enables us to cope with the insights of others. While avoiding the charge of 'woolliness', we need a theological basis for our encounter with other Christians which makes it possible for us to discover the truth in them without denying the truth we have already found for ourselves. Such a basis is essential if there is to be integrity in the search for unity.

The beginnings of such a foundation may be found in the notion of paradox or dialectic. Truth held in tension need not arise out of any intellectual laziness or misguided sentiment, but from the mystery of God which cannot be contained within human language and experience. In pointing towards the divine mystery, two truths held in tension may bring us closer than one truth on its own. Historically, the best example of this is the doctrine of the Trinity, where we hold three claims about God in tension at the same time. Such a method enables us to recognize the truth in others and provides a basis for seeing how their truth and our truth might relate to each other. The encounter reminds us that this is no abstract exercise, but involves people and communities which must be reconciled in love.

When we ask about the something or the someone which keeps the diverse insights or divergent traditions in tension, we find the task an elusive one. The attempt is currently being made to use the Nicene Creed as a vehicle for such an agreement in theological affirmation. But the problem arises when some demand a more detailed creed, while others express reservations about using a creed at all. Again we are back to that elusive *something* which we discover and recognize in the encounter with one another. It may be the life of prayer, it may be a spiritual experience, such as charismatic worship, or it may be a common concern for the agonies of the world. Some alliances will be made on the basis of one or more of these shared features, but none of them will serve for *all* Christians. This is where we are driven to see an allegiance to Jesus[1] as the uniting factor amongst Christians. It is *he* who gives the church its identity, uniting diverse traditions and various gifts in a pattern which gains meaning from his love.

So-called 'spiritual unity' is not enough, for we are summoned to be disciples in *this* world. We must take the structures of the church seriously and we must take the notion of incarnation seriously. We need to live the unity which is a part of the gospel and this is expressed in terms of the Kingdom of God when we say that the church must be a servant, a sign and a foretaste of the Kingdom. In so far as that kingdom is ultimately founded on God's shalom, we can see how visible unity in the church is an important part of the life as well as the mission of the church.

Our concern for mission again forces us back to face the issue of unity and division. The credibility of the church is demonstrated both by a proper stewardship of material resources and by the living witness to a gospel of love. Shared mission also provides opportunities for encounter in action where Christians can grow together by acting together. The word *ecumenical* is about both the world and the church: as the Easter people, the church becomes more truly itself as it lives under the Lordship of Christ. Its good news of reconciling love and forgiving hope becomes incarnate in the sacramental community, which, in turn, becomes a sign of hope for a despairing world.

This is the vision which summons us, the call that leads us from closed prejudices to an open future. But to share the vision is one thing, to discover how it is to be lived is another. Questions abound, but the strength of our vision will make us more able to face the difficulties and struggles. This is the importance of the present task. A strong theological basis for the search for unity will provide us with some of the resources needed to cope with the unknown, the uncertain and the unclear.

Yet *how* questions remain, and while leaving a detailed response to them to other writers in other places, it is right to ask here if there are any pointers which arise out of the reflections we have undertaken. In particular, we can be justified in asking 'What is unity? If there is diversity in unity, then what kind of unity, what kind of relationships, what kind of church structures, can we envisage?'

What is Unity?

It is, of course, more difficult to give a detailed description of unity than it is to affirm the principle that unity is important. For a number of reasons, this is not as vague as it might seem.

First, we cannot predict the pattern of unity in a detailed way in the abstract because unity will always need to be situational. Different contexts – the missionary situation, the local culture, the history of relationships, outside pressures and local personalities – will all play a part in the *form* unity will take. We have seen that the diversity in the New Testament was, at least partly, a response to different cultural and religious situations. This must always be so, and the form unity will take in a particular place should be influenced by the local conditions.

The second reason follows from the first. We cannot predict in advance what form unity will take, because we do not know which parties will be involved. If unity is the uniting of A + B + C, then we need to know who A and B and C are before we can begin to guess at the nature of their unity. While we can hope for the unity of all the churches, we must acknowledge that it isn't that simple, and the churches which are involved in any particular place will inevitably affect the nature of the unity. This is a clear lesson from Local Ecumenical Projects in England, where the variety encourages us towards a far more dynamic and creative understanding of unity than would be the case if we were to expect only one definition of what unity means.

Thirdly, to prescribe in advance the form unity should take would be to indulge in ideological planning rather than Christian hope. The search for unity ought to involve faith, hope and love. The hope is given to us in the call of God, love will be the means by which the partners will grow in unity, and faith should place the search in God's gracious hands, without wanting to know the details of the future in advance. If we must use pictures to help our understanding of unity, then we are more likely to find them in the area of human relationships than we are in mechanics. The process of growing in unity is one of increasing trust and acceptance as well as learning and sharing. It is not a mechanical process of adding on components.

In human relationships all the partners are affected and changed. Something new is the result. This something new has grown out of the old – the people are the same people, but they have been changed. So, in looking forward to unity, we cannot prescribe what that unity will look like without stifling the scope of trust or limiting the initiatives of the Spirit. This is why the picture of pilgrimage is such a good one.

However, it might be argued that these comments suggest a local understanding of unity rather than a universal one. This is true, but it is presented in the knowledge that our understanding of unity will differ at each *level* of the church just as it will from place to place. For example, the form of unity which could include the Roman Catholic Church worldwide may well be very different from the kind of unity it is able to be involved with at national, diocesan or local levels. There is no blueprint which can be applied to all levels, for each level has its own needs, opportunities and difficulties. A future unity will need to include the relationship between different local levels as well as the relationship of the local to the universal.

Thus the attempt to paint pictures of a future unity will need to take account of the variety of contexts and the variety of levels. There are things which can be said about the world scene, but they are different from what can be said about the variety of local possibilities.

133

A phrase which was introduced into international Faith and Order discussions a few years ago was *conciliar fellowship*. This was the subject of a number of Faith and Order meetings and consultations[2] and was included in the report 'What Unity Requires', which was accepted and recommended to the churches by the fifth assembly of the World Council of Churches in Nairobi in 1975. That report included the following statement:

> 'The one church is to be envisioned as a conciliar fellowship of local chuches which are themselves truly united. In this conciliar fellowship, each local church possesses, in communion with the others, the fulness of catholicity, witnesses to the same apostolic faith, and therefore recognizes the others as belonging to the same church of Christ and guided by the same Spirit . . . they are bound together because they have received the same baptism and share the same eucharist; they recognize each other's members and ministries. They are one in their common commitment to confess the Gospel of Christ by proclamation and service to the world. To this end, each church aims at maintaining sustained and sustaining relationships with her sister churches, expressed in conciliar gatherings whenever required for the fulfilment of their common calling.'[3]

There is much in this statement which is lacking in detail, but it is an attempt to provide some clear principles, while making provision for flexible adapation to local circumstances. Although this model seems to offer a pattern which would allow for unity with diversity it must be recognized that some churches find the diversity easier to accept than others. This underlines an important requirement of possible future patterns of unity. Is it possible to develop patterns of unity which might have the ecclesial equivalent of a gear system? There are churches whose relationships within their denomination are fairly loose, (eg. Congregationalists), just as there are churches which have closer lines of authority and a tight ecclesial structure. We need to search for models of unity which enable different churches to relate to each other according to their own ecclesiological ability or will. It is unreasonable to expect a denomination to enter a more formal and binding relationship with other denominations than the relationships which link its own congregations. Again, are we talking about an intermediate stage, where a degree of untidiness can be accepted so long as we are moving forward to a more complete catholicity, or are we describing the inevitable and permanent untidiness of human community?

Signposts

Talk of conciliar fellowship can lead to the question of visible and invisible unity. For example, we might enquire into the difference between a federated council, such as a council of churches, and the kind of conciliar fellowship which would enable full eucharistic sharing and recognition of members and ministries. Confessing a common faith will be important, but what of styles of worship, authority in teaching, joint decision-making and the other practical aspects of shared discipline, which identify a community as *one* community, rather than several communities which co-exist and sometimes co-operate? Theological reflection is needed not only on each of these issues but on the process itself – the interim stages through which the churches will need to move. We need a theology of ecumenical *movement*[4] which makes sense of the inevitable untidiness of a pilgrim people.

Another issue which we must face at this point is the relationship of unity to structure. We have argued that *visible* unity is needed in order to incarnate the gospel of reconciliation and in order to live the communal aspects of divine love. But does this need a structure of unity or can it be expressed by ad hoc initiatives and personal friendships? The personal dimension is important, but we must claim that the *structures* of the churches need to be brought under the judgement of our hope as we ask, 'What is there in the church structures which hinders growth towards unity and human renewal?' While we need to exercise love, we need to protect that love and provide it with the support and environment which it deserves – just as in human sexual and parental love we provide the framework of marriage and family. This challenges us to face the question of commitment. If it has the nature of a divine imperative, unity needs to be accepted as a priority and expressed in terms of a commitment, not only to the ideal of unity, but to the particular partners in unity that have been entrusted to us by God.[5]

Goals are important for providing perspectives, but they often need to be accompanied by other aids to navigation. One aid, originally proposed some years ago, is called 'The Five Cs' and offers a scale by which we can judge the state of relationships between the churches.[6]

COMPETITION

CO-EXISTENCE

CO-OPERATION

COMMITMENT

COMMUNION

Church relationships may straddle several of these stages, in which case the scale enables us to identify which areas of church life are more or less ecumenically advanced.

Seeing the growth towards unity on such a scale presents us with two important warnings. First, the move towards unity is not inevitable. The hope which we have before us is God's future for the church and for the world, but the human freedom which he has given us means that his will can be frustrated. The very sinfulness of the world and the divisions of the church are testimony to this.

The hope before us is a divine summons, but it is the summons of a partent, a friend, a lover.

The second warning is that not all unity is good. There are false examples of unity both in the world and in the church. History is littered with attempts to enforce unity by violence and oppression. Such unity is a denial, and not an establishing, of the Kingdom. We have attempted to expound the theme of unity within the framework of the Christian gospel and this means that any unity which is a denial of that gospel is a false unity. The church gains its identity as the Easter people by living under the Lordship of Christ. Coercion, violence and fear are methods which deny the one who washed his disciples' feet, rode a donkey and died on a cross. He came to announce liberty to the captive, so his people cannot endorse unity by imprisoning those whom he has set free.

Invitation to Pilgrimage

The British Inter-Church Process of the 1980's, *Not Strangers but Pilgrims* is just one example of using the metaphor of pilgrimage for the search for unity. It is a powerful picture and one which has an interesting and ecumenical pedigree. [7] In an age of inter-continental travel, it is easy to forget some of the aspects of the religious pilgrimage, where the journey was a vital part of the total experience.

Pilgrimage is not like tourism, which sets out to see the sights. It has set before it a significant goal, one that has meaning for the traveller but has not been seen. The road is an unknown road, walked in faith. While not strictly pilgrimage, the stories of Abraham's call, the exodus wanderings and the return from exile are biblical themes which Christian devotion has linked with actual and spiritual pilgrimages. Thus the idea of *promise* becomes very important. *Effort* is expended on the long journey, but the end has been given by God, and so the whole journey and arrival are a means of grace. If we continue the picture of ancient pilgrimages, then we can introduce the *slowness* of the journey (walking pace?) and the dangers and uncertainties of the journey. If Chaucer's *Canterbury Tales* are anything to go by, then we can add *companionship* and *sharing* as dimensions of the pilgrimage, though these were probably more for mutual support and protection than for entertainment.

So we are called to share in an ecumenical pilgrimage. We are called to share in a journey that has been prepared for, undertaken and pioneered by others who have gone before us. The goal is known, though it has not been seen. Companions have been invited and the journey will involve risks, hardships and excitement. Readers will need to determine whether or not the reflections of this book lead them to identify the invitation as the voice of God, or the vain dreams of a wilful humanity. We must be concerned with faithfulness as well as faith, for the God who calls comes to us in the Jesus who gives himself for us and says, 'Follow me'.

> 'Lord God, we thank you
> for calling us into the company
> of those who trust in Christ
> and seek to obey his will.
> May your Spirit guide and strengthen us
> in mission and service to your world;
> And may we be strangers no longer
> but pilgrims together on the way to your
> Kingdom. Amen.'[8]

Notes

1. While 'Jesus is Lord' has been used widely in this book as a formula to unite Christians, we must recognize that its origin is in a particular cultural context viz. early Hellenistic Christianity. If it is to be a unifying confession then we need to see it as a symbol for the priority and authority of Jesus which may, in different contexts, be expressed in different ways. Eg. see J. Pelikan, 'Jesus through the Centuries: His place in the history of culture' (Yale) 1985.

2. For 'Conciliar fellowship' see 'Conciliarity and the future of the Ecumenical Movement: Louvain 1971' (Geneva) 1971; L. Vischer, ed. 'What kind of Unity?' (Geneva) 1974 pp119-130; 'Uniting in Hope: Accra 1974' (Geneva) 1975 pp110-123; D. Paton, ed., 'Breaking Down Barriers: Nairobi 1975' (London and Grand Rapids) 1976 pp57-69.

3. 'Breaking Barriers' p60.

4. See W.A. Visser 't Hooft, 'The Pressure of our Common Calling' (London) 1959.

5. See 'Uniting in Hope' pp120-123.

6. The scale was originally suggested by John Nicholson, a former Ecumenical Officer for England of the British Council of Churches. An example of 'The Five Cs' is printed in M. Kinnamon, ed., 'Towards Visible Unity: Commission of Faith and Order, Lima 1982' (Geneva) 1982 pp226.

7. The journey to a sacred site is a form of religious activity found in other religions, but it has gained a new dimension with the Christian doctrine of incarnation which has enabled places, people and material images to become

sources of encouragement. The practice which flourished in the medieval Catholic Church, but which was discouraged by the Reformers, found a new, if metaphorical, life in the writings of the Puritan Independent John Bunyan.

8. 'Churches Together in Pilgrimage' BCC/CTS (London) 1989 p8.

APPENDICES

QUESTIONS FOR GROUP DISCUSSION AND PERSONAL REFLECTION

Introduction
1. What do *you* think about the ecumenical movement? Do you see yourself as a supporter, a critic or someone with reservations? What are the reasons for your present views?
2. What experience have you had of local unity? What are your hopes for your own situation? What would you like to see happen in the next ten years and the next two years?
3. What do you see as the main obstacles to church unity?

Song of Creation
1. What has the word *ecumenical* meant to you and, after reading this chapter, what do you think its relevance to be to the needs of the world?
2. What part does Christian hope play in the search for unity?
3. How does the confession 'Jesus is Lord' affect the lifestyle of the church and what are its implications for the relationships *between* Christians?

Biblical Reflections
1. Read Ephesians 2.11-22. How are peace with God and peace with one another linked? What does this mean for the preaching of the gospel?
2. Read 1 Corinthians 12-14. Is this relevant to the differences *between* the churches or only to the variety *within* the churches?
3. Read 1 John 4.19-21. How does love find expression between groups and churches?

Multiple History
1. What do you know about the origins of the church to which you belong? What were the reasons for its formation and how has it changed over the years?
2. What does your church 'stand for' which makes it different from other denominations?
3. What does the phrase 'legitimate diversity' mean and how would you apply it to Christian belief, worship, organization and mission?

Confessing One Lord

1. What is the difference between diversity and division?
2. 'All in each place' – read again the statement for New Delhi. How united can a local church be?
3. 'Jesus Christ is both at the centre and at the boundary of Christian identity.' What does this mean? How many different ways can you explain the phrase, 'Jesus is Lord'?

Truth in Tension

1. What does the doctrine of the Trinity tell us about the nature of Christian truth?
2. How does an awareness of the greatness of God and of our own human limitations provide us with the basis for an ecumenical theology?
3. What is the difference between openness and woolliness?

Visible Versus Invisible

1. Is 'invisible unity' possible?
2. What does the doctrine of the incarnation have to say for the way in which denominations relate to one another?
3. How can *your* church be a foretaste of the kingdom of God?

Inside Out

1. Why do stewardship and ecumenism belong together?
2. What is the challenge of credibility for the churches in your locality?
3. What does ecumenism have to do with mission? What are the practical and theological links?

Signposts

1. Is unity the will of God?
2. What does unity mean for those parts of the church that you know?
3. Pilgrims together: how do we move from co-operation to commitment and from there to communion?

II

BIBLIOGRAPHY

List of Books and Articles Cited in the Text

M.L. Appold, 'The Oneness Motif in the Fourth Gospel' (Tubingen) 1976.

'Baptism, Eucharist and Ministry' (Geneva) 1982.

C.K. Barrett, 'The Epistle to the Romans' (London) 1957.

K. Barth, 'Church Dogmatics' I.1. ET (Edinburgh) 1936.

M. Barth, 'Ephesians 4-6' (New York) 1974.

P.L. Berger, 'The Social Reality of Religion' (London) 1967.

T.F. Best, ed. 'Faith and Renewal: Reports and Documents of the Commission on Faith and Order, Stavanger 1985' (Geneva) 1986.

L. Boff, 'Ecclesiogenesis' ET (London) 1986.

M. Bordeaux, 'Risen Indeed' (London) 1983.

J. Bluck, 'Everyday Ecumenism: Can you take the World church home?' (Geneva) 1987.

R.E. Brown, 'The Church the Apostles Left Behind' (London) 1984.

R.E. Brown, 'The Gospel According to John vol II' (New York) 1970.

R.M. Brown, 'The Ecumenical Revolution' (London) 1967.

E. Brunner, 'The Word and the World': SCM Press (London) 1931.

J.T. Christian, 'A History of the Baptists' (Nashville) 1922.

'The Churches survey their Task: the Report of the Conference at Oxford, July 1937, on Church, Community, and State' (London) 1937.

'Conciliarity and the future of the Ecumenical Movement' (Geneva) 1971.

Y. Congar, 'Diversity and Communion' ET (London) 1984.

J.M. Cramp, 'Baptist History: from the foundation of the Christian Church to the present day' (London) 1871.

F.L. Cross, 'The Oxford Dictionary of the Christian Church' (London) 1957.

J.G. Davies, 'Members One of Another' (London) 1958.

J.G. Davies, 'The Early Church' (London) 1965.

R.E. Davies, 'The Church in our Times: An Ecumenical History from a British Perspective' (London) 1979.

C.H. Dodd, 'The Parables of the Kingdom' (London) 1935.

J.D. Dunn, 'Unity and Diversity in the New Testament: An inquiry into the character of earliest Christianity' (London) 1977.

G. Ebeling, 'The Word of God and Tradition' ET (London) 1968.

H.E. Fey, ed., 'The Ecumenical Advance – A History of the Ecumenical Movement vol 2. 1948-1968' 2nd Ed. (Geneva) 1986.

H.C. Frend, 'The Rise of Christianity' (London) 1984.

R.H. Fuller, 'New Testament Trajectories and Biblical Authority', in 'Studia Evangelica' VII (Berlin) 1982.

D. Gill, ed., 'Gathered for Life: Official Report, Sixth Assembly of the World Council of Churches' (Geneva and Grand Rapids) 1983.

'Giving Account of Hope', The Ecumenical Review, XXXX, 1 January 1979.

'God's Reign and Our Unity: The report of the Anglican-Reformed International Commission 1981-1984' (London) 1984.

N. Goodall, 'The Uppsala Report' (Geneva) 1968.

B. Haymes, 'A Question of Identity; Reflections on Baptist Principles and Practice' (Yorkshire Baptist Association) 1986.

Hilary of Poitiers, 'On the Trinity' in W. Sanday, ed., 'A Select Library of the Nicene and Post Nicene Fathers of the Christian Church' (Oxford) 1899 vol IX.

A.M. Hunter, 'Interpreting the Parables' (London) 1960.

J. Jeremias, 'The Parables of Jesus' ET (London) 1963.

John of Damascus, 'Exposition of the Orthodox Faith' in W. Sanday, ed., 'A Select Library of the Nicene and Post Nicene Fathers of the Christian Church' (Oxford) 1899 vol IX.

C. Jones, G. Wainwright and E. Yarnold, ed., 'The study of Liturgy' (London) 1978.

E. Kasemann, 'Essays on New Testament Themes' ET (London) 1964.

E. Kasemann, 'New Testament Questions of Today' ET (London) 1969.

J. Kent, 'The Unacceptable Face: The Modern Church in the Eyes of the Historian' (London) 1987.

M. Kinnamon and T.F. Best, ed., 'Called to be One: United Churches and the Ecumenical Movement' (Geneva) 1985.

M. Kinnamon, ed., 'Towards Visible Unity: Commission on Faith and Order, Lima, 1982: Study Papers and Reports' (Geneva) 1982.

H. Kung, 'The Church Maintained in Truth: A Theological Meditation' ET (London) 1980.

H.G. Link, ed., 'Apostolic Faith Today: A Handbook for Study' (Geneva) 1985.

H.G. Link, ed., 'Confessing our Faith around the world' vols 1-4 (Geneva) 1982-85.

J. Lochman, 'The Faith We Confess' (Philadelphia) 1984.

J. Macquarrie, 'In Search of Deity: An Essay in Dialiectical Theism' The Gifford Lectures for 1983-84: SCM Press (London) 1984.

T.W. Manson in M. Black, ed., 'On Paul and Jesus' (London) 1963.

R.P. Martin, 'Reconciliation: A study of Paul's Theology' (London) 1981.

J. Matthews, 'The Unity Scene' (London) 1986.

H. Meyer and L. Vischer, ed., 'Growth in Agreement' (Geneva) 1984.

J. Moltmann, 'The Church in the Power of the Spirit' ET (London) 1977.

J. Moltmann, 'Theology of Hope' ET: SCM Press (London) 1967.

L. Newbigin, 'The Light has Come: An exposition of the Fourth Gospel' (Grand Rapids) 1982.

'The New Delhi Report' (London) 1962.

N.A. Nissiotis in G. Limouris, ed., 'Church, Kingdom, World: The Church as Mystery and Prophetic Sign' (Geneva) 1986.

H.J.M. Nouwen, 'Behold the Beauty of the Lord: Praying with Icons' (Notre Dame) 1987.

A. Papaderos, 'Ecumenism as Celebration' in P. Webb, 'Faith and Faithfulness: Essays on Contemporary Ecumenical Themes, A tribute to Philip A. Potter' (Geneva) 1984.

D. Paton, ed., 'Breaking Down Barriers: Nairobi 1975' (London and Grand Rapids) 1976.

J. Pelikan, 'Jesus through the Centuries: His place in the history of culture' (Yale) 1985.

R. Robertson, 'The Sociological Interpretation of Religion' (Oxford) 1970.

R. Rouse and S.C. Neill, ed., 'A History of the Ecumenical Movement vol 1, 1517-1948' 3rd Ed. (Geneva) 1986.

R. Schnackenburg, 'The Gospel According to John vol III' ET (London) 1982.

E. Schweitzer, 'The Letter to the Colossians' ET (London) 1982.

'Sharing in One Hope' (Geneva) 1978.

S. Sykes, 'The Identity of Christianity' (London) 1984.

S. Sykes, 'The Integrity of Anglicanism' (London) 1978.

Mary Tanner, 'Where are we? Where are we going? The work of Faith and Order in the 1980's' in J.H.Y. Briggs, ed., 'Faith, Heritage and Witness: A supplement to the Baptist Quarterly published in honour of Dr. W.M.S. West', Baptist Historical Society (London) 1987.

J.V. Taylor, 'Enough is Enough' (London) 1975.

R.S. Thomas, 'Collected Poems 1948-1968' (London) 1973.

M. Thurian and G. Wainwright, 'Baptism and Eucharist: Ecumenical Convergence in Celebration' (Geneva and Grand Rapids) 1983.

'Uniting in Hope: Accra 1974' (Geneva) 1975.

Second Vatican Council 'Decree on Ecumenism'.

J. Vincent 'The Alternative Church' (Belfast) 1976.

L. Vischer, ed., 'What kind of Unity?' (Geneva) 1974.

W.A. Visser 't Hooft, 'The Meaning of Ecumenical' (London) 1953.

W.A. Visser 't Hooft, 'The Pressure of our Common Calling' (London) 1959.

G. Wainwright, 'Doxology: A Systematic Theology' (London) 1980.

B. Wilson, 'Religion in Secular Society' (London) 1966.

D. Winter, 'Hope in Captivity' (London) 1977.